W9-CSV-596

STREETPROOFING: GENTLY AND CREATIVELY

Sharon E. McKay

Royce Publications

© 1985 by Royce Publications

Typesetting by Jay Tee Graphics Ltd.
Cover photo by Stephen McKay

Published by Royce Publications
90 Ronson Drive
Rexdale, Ontario M9W 1C1

Canadian Cataloguing in Publication Data

ISBN: 0-7740-3836-5

Printed and bound in Canada
1 2 3 4 5 85 89 88 87 86

© COPYRIGHT 1985 AND PUBLISHED BY
ROYCE PUBLISHING COMPANY
TORONTO — CANADA
PRINTED IN CANADA

to david macleod, husband and friend

ACKNOWLEDGMENTS

To my parents Dorothy and Ian and to my brothers Stephen and Dave — friends and babysitters par excellence.

My thanks to Liz Watson and staff, W. Ross MacDonald School; Dava Parr and staff, Ernest C. Dury School; Rhonda Collis, Peel Family Education Centre; Erica Redman, parenting specialist; Hamilton Cue, *Toronto Parent Magazine*; Valerie Wilson, YMCA, Brampton.

I also am grateful to Adele Wootton, Managing Editor of Royce Publications, Leslie Wylie, Editor and to Helen Wagenaar, typist extraordinaire, who just kept going.

"Canadians are deeply concerned about the need to provide better protection for sexually-abused and exploited children and youths. This strongly-held concern is national in scope. It cuts across all social, religious, and political boundaries. It encompasses all forms of sexual abuse of the child, whether this involves sexual assault, juvenile prostitution or the making of child pornography."

Sexual Offenses Against Children in Canada: Report of the Committee on Sexual Offenses Against Children and Youth; the Minister of National Health and Welfare, 1984

Contents

	Introduction	X
I	The Basics	1
II	The Rules	14
III	Lost and Found	20
IV	A Word about Handicapped Children	33
V	Creative Streetproofing from Birth to Three	35
VI	Creative Streetproofing from Three to Six	45
VII	Creative Streetproofing from Six to Ten	58
VIII	Sexism	72
IX	Dressing Children	79
X	Street Smarts	83
XI	Bullies	88
XII	Making Friends	93
XIII	Abusers	95
XIV	The Tools of the Molester	101
XV	Listen to your Children	108
XVI	Talking to your Children	113
XVII	Using the World Around Us	118
XVIII	Storytime	126
XIX	Incest	141
XX	Child Stealing and Non-Custodial Abductions	147
XXI	Latchkey Kids	152
XXII	Babysitters	158
	Conclusion	165
	Appendix	166

Introduction

The normal gestation period of a fetus is ten years. Forget the medical evidence to the contrary, and ask an expert — an expectant mother who waits and waits. She suffers through fat jokes and unsolicited advice from taxi drivers and companion elevator riders, she reads about her weight in parenting books, trots off dutifully to pre-natal, exercise, and parenting classes. All this, surely, takes longer than a mere nine months!

Then the magic happens! Suddenly, after eighteen to twenty-four hours of hard labour and cheerful encouragement from a hyperventilated husband and a platoon of skinny nurses, a baby. A Boy? A Girl? Oh, God, a human being! Hard-core atheists look upward, "So, this is a miracle! Not bad."

"A baby, my baby!" And the outside world fades away. The mortgage may be up for renewal, the car about to be repossessed. The country may be on the brink of financial collapse with the world steadily looping toward yet another holocaust; yet, the planet at large is a blur. Here are Mother and Child, that timeless picture of civility! And we make promises to our infants, "I'll keep you safe. I'll love you forever."

Then, slowly at first, our re-entry begins. We pick up a newspaper and find a two-inch blurb on a back page, bottom left-hand corner, "Child Abuse on the Rise," "Toddler Abducted from Backyard," or worse still, "Infant Abandoned in Garbage Can." Such crimes have always been around, but in the past, during pre-parenthood, we just scanned the news, tisk-tisked and wondered whether the world was going to hell in a handbasket.

It is different now. We are different now. The idea creeps into our heads that someone might harm our baby may be so repugnant and overwhelming that we don't even think of prevention. That is a normal reaction but, at some point, we realize that our children's safety has become more important than our own sensitivities.

Most of us are sympathetic to the problems of children but sympathy is, for the most part, a learned emotion. Now we have a new emotion to contend with — empathy. We can feel the agony of parents who have lost a child, we can feel the pain of an abused, abducted or molested child. It is gut-wrenching. True, empathy is not the sole preserve of caring parents, of course not. However, this is a book for parents, those parents who look at their infant and say, "If anything happens to you, kid, they had better dig two graves!"

In writing this book, I had many hopes, primarily to evoke thought and, from time to time, a smile. I speak to parents like myself who have been overwhelmed by statistics, by the battery of information on child abuse from every possible source, and by reports on abductions and sexual molestations.

As a parent and researcher I have, over the past years, attended many workshops and seminars on child protection. I have listened to criminologists, sociologists, social workers and to members of children's protection groups, clubs, and organizations. Like many of the other parents sitting in the audience, I emerged feeling paralyzed with fear, confused and, ultimately, helpless.

I have listened to people tell me that unless I drill countless, unexplained, dogmatic rules into my child's head I am a bad mother, deliberately putting my child at risk. On more than one occasion, husband David and I left a class, hanging on to one another, shaken, vowing that our child would never be a child abuse statistic. We would teach him. Yes, we would. But how?

I remember during one such presentation, a mother standing up and recanting the following story in a calm, matter-of-fact voice:

"We had just moved into a new area from across the country. Our six-year-old was out playing on the front lawn with some children when a car pulled up. A woman opened the door and began calling, 'Come here, come here.' My son started to scream. He became confused and unsure of his surroundings, sat on the ground yelling, 'That lady is trying to steal me. Help! Help!' We ran outside. It took us awhile to calm him down. There was another neighbour across the street mowing his lawn. He was witness to the entire incident. Apparently, the woman in the car was trying to get her stray cat into the car."

After a brief pause, the woman added:

"Maybe our son is a little paranoid, maybe he did overreact; but I'd rather have him this way, over-protected, than the other way."

What is the "other way?" Does it necessarily follow that the opposite to paranoid is willing, compliant? Or can we say that the reverse of paranoia is secure, rational, confident?

What do I want for my son? Do I want him to grow up full of fear, doubting everyone who crosses his path? Will he develop to his full potential if he is filled with anxiety? Is this the trade-off I am forced to make to keep my child safe? I love my son more than my life, my love for him is greater than any I have ever experienced. Am I now to take that love, and sacrifice to it his development, all under the auspicious umbrella of protecting him for his own good? Who am I protecting — myself from "mega-hurt" or my child from danger?

What are the long-range implications of teaching our children rules such as, "Don't let anyone touch your private parts?" Will this rule fall naturally to the wayside one day, or will it inhibit individuals from enjoying normal, healthy sexual relations? I don't want my child to be the test case.

When we dogmatically and repeatedly tell our children, "Don't talk to strangers," we enforce the rule with innuendoes and vague intimations. To whom will they go for help when they are lost and alone? Will ingrained mistrust of their surroundings be conducive to the development of their full social potentials? The ability to converse, to deal with people, to speak in public will not be an attribute in the future. It will become a necessary skill. Will a child naturally shrug off the old childhood rules and start afresh on his/her twenty-first birthday?

No, we don't want our children talking to everyone they meet, nor do we want them to feel obliged to be polite and considerate at the expense of their safety. We want them to develop discretion and find a balance between the two opposing poles.

We need rules. We need points of reference. Teaching children how to protect themselves can never be done in a vacuum. The rules we make must be related to their surroundings, based on reason and commonsense.

We all want our children to be safe. As parents, grandparents and guardians, we are looking for answers. We are in a state of confusion. Along comes "streetproofing," seemingly the word that will provide the answer. It is not the answer. There is no *one* answer. Nor can any one individual or organization guarantee every child's safe conduct to his/her twenty-first birthday. But we are all trying. We are all scrambling to find a method, a way to ensure our child's well-being. It is a valid quest, but just as there are no specific or pat answers, no one is an authority or an expert on the subject. The police are not, nor are teachers, social workers, members of children's organizations or authors of streetproofing books.

And just as there are good reasons to teach children about their world, their bodies, and streetproofing in general, increasingly, there are bad or wrong reasons. A weary mother of two boys under seven, best articulated this by stating:

"If they learn this streetproofing stuff, it would save me a bundle in babysitters."

Another mother of a six-year-old mirrored the same sentiment:

"I just want to make sure my daughter will not go with a stranger. If she understands that, I won't have to walk her to the bus stop every morning."

Parents are the protectors. No amount of streetproofing can ever change or diminish that role. No matter how aware a child is, no matter how bright or discerning, all children need our vigilance and constant protection.

Each of us must do our own research, seeking information from diverse sources. Then we must assume our responsibilities. Over the years, as a speaker and columnist on the topic of child protection, I have repeatedly heard parents make the statement, "My children get all of this in school." What they leave unsaid but adamantly imply is, "and thank God, I wouldn't touch this stuff with a ten-foot pole." During a seminar at a well-established religious school, a bewildered new principal told me, "I received a call today from a furious parent. Her daughter had been caught shoplifting and she wanted to know what I was going to do about it!" Teaching children about honesty, about their world, about themselves, ultimately is our responsibility, not the community's, not the school's, nor the church's.

Here is a statement that has become a cliché: "Only you know your child best." It is, nevertheless, true that we know our children and their environment, and if we pay attention, we also know their fears and stresses. As parents we are in the best position to talk to them about streetproofing, about sexual molestation, about how to cross the street.

This is a book for parents who do not feel joy and excitement while watching their child trot off to school for the first time; who lie in bed, unable to sleep, imagining the unimaginable. It is also a book for parents who don't believe in all that "streetproofing stuff" because it "scares children more than it protects them."

This book is meant to be the beginning or the middle of your information gathering venture. There simply is no end to it. I hope you will find it useful. Pick out what you need, what applies to your family's circumstances. Devise your own plan of protection and commit yourself to it. Initially, this may seem a horrendous and exhausting task, and you may well wonder, "Isn't all that streetproofing stuff just media hype?"

Judge for yourself. Here are the statistics:

- At some time during their lives, about one in two females and one in three males were victims of one or more unwanted sexual acts. These acts include being exposed to, being sexually threatened, being touched on a sexual part of the body, attempts of assault or being sexually assaulted.
- About four in five of these unwanted sexual acts had been first committed against these persons when they were children or youths.
- Four in 100 of young females have been raped.
- Two in 100 of young persons have experienced attempts or actual acts of unwanted anal penetration by a penis, or by means of objects or fingers.
- Acts of exposure constitute the largest single category of sexual offenses committed against children. Documented cases reveal that such acts were followed by sexual assault.
- Three in five sexually-abused children have been threatened or physically coerced by their assailants.

Young victims are as likely to be threatened or forced to engage in sexual acts by persons relatively close in age as well as by older persons.

- Few young victims were physically injured; substantially more suffered emotional harm.
- About one in four assailants is a family member or a person in a position of trust; about half are friends or acquaintances, and about one in six is a stranger.
- Virtually all assailants are males, one in 100 is a female.
- A majority of victims or their families do not seek assistance from public services. When they do, they turn most often to the police and doctors.
- Over two in five of all sexual assault homicides are committed against children aged fifteen and younger. Children are victims of three in four convicted sexual offenders found to be dangerous on sentencing by courts.

Sexual Offences Against Children in Canada,
Summary, The Minister of Justice
and Attorney General of Canada,
The Minister of National Health and Welfare,
Government of Canada, 1984.

It is inevitable that when one report is issued, a second and third one will appear to counter it. But statistics change and subsequent reports may suggest that the abuse of children has diminished. We may credit our vigilance, providing our interest in the subject does not wane.

One thing is certain, children are still being abused right now, they have been abused in the past and unless the world does a somersault, they will be abused in the future. Is this to suggest that nothing can be done? No. As parents concerned with the healthy development of all children, it is immaterial to us whether one child in five or one in a hundred is abused. What matters is that child abuse must *never* happen.

Childhood is not a state of repose or naiveté but a period of growth and development. If we truly wanted to keep our children out of harm's way, we could most certainly do that by locking them in a room and not letting them out until they have come of age. A paranoid parent will produce a fearful child. At best, fear may protect a child from falling off a building, but at the other end of the scale, it clouds the mind and paralyzes the body. We want to teach our children to respect their environment, not fear it. We want them to be assertive, not aggressive. However, before we can accomplish that, we must first take stock of what we are trying to achieve when we streetproof a child.

Gentle and creative streetproofing is an attempt to encourage children to follow a path of common-sense safety, by helping them develop the ability to make decisions and follow their own instincts. By definition, to streetproof children is to instill in them a healthy respect for potentially dangerous situations, and to provide them with effective means to identify and react to such situations whenever or wherever they may feel threatened.

As the statistics show, children are more often in danger in their own homes than on the street, and this occasionally makes the term "streetproofing" sound misleading. Some of us may prefer the word "homeproofing," but what we want as parents are practical and implementable suggestions.

Streetproofing is positive because it is preventative. If we look upon it in this manner, neither fear nor paranoia will ever be an issue. Let me again emphasize that we want to raise happy and aware children. Should streetproofing ever interfere with that, backtrack, rethink and present the material in a different manner. If a child shows signs of stress, drop the subject. Nothing, I repeat, nothing is more important than to make him/her feel secure within his/her own world. Gentle and creative streetproofing is meant to increase that security, not diminish it. Streetproofing is part of parenting, and parenting requires work, thought and care. There are no shortcuts, no hard and fast rules, no hot tips, nor ten easy lessons to be drilled into the heads of unsuspecting children while their behinds are bolted to the living room sofa.

Streetproofing: Gently and Creatively is a collection of ideas. You may not always agree with them, but to disagree requires thought, and thought is all I ask for. It has always been my hope that parents come to my seminars with ten questions to be answered and leave with twenty different ones. That same hope persists with this book. It was written for parents who, like myself, want the best of both worlds for their children — safety and confidence.

I

THE BASICS

We are trying to do much more than protect our children. We are trying to protect their CHILD-HOOD.

Streetproofing is a very realistic discipline that can only work if it fits in with your particular way of looking at the world. Streetproofing cannot be applied to children like a coat of paint. Only you can decide what is best for *your* son or daughter. What then are the characteristics of a streetproofed child?

Developing Self-esteem

First and foremost, a child needs to feel confident in herself. She needs to have trust in her abilities and receive trust from at least one loving adult source.

While the topic of enhancing self-esteem easily could fill all the pages of this book, it also is necessary to point out how many parents stifle the development of self-esteem in their children.

A primary concern is to make sure their first-born is not spoiled. If baby cries in her crib but has been changed and fed, then baby had better learn the facts of life, "You are not the only one around, kiddo," and "I'm not here to cater to you, Miss." At three, four or five months, Baby is not yet aware that if Mommy leaves the room, she has not left this planet. Poor Baby! She cannot even vocalize her desires in an acceptable manner. Why, she can't even talk! So she cries. What a rude Baby! But maybe Baby is lonely? Maybe Baby needs a hug?

Many parents say with pride, "Well, she cried the first night for 45 minutes, and the second night for 30 minutes and by the third night, she only cried for ten minutes and now look, she does not cry at all!" Good for the parents. They now have a docile baby who has indeed learned her lesson. She has learned that she is not all that important in the scheme of things. Her desires and needs come second to everyone else's, and her resources to obtain help are limited.

In the words of Dodson, author of the book, *How to Parent*, "Spoiling is for fruit, not children," and to quote LaLeche League, an international organization for nursing mothers, "Crying is good for the lungs like bleeding is good for the veins." If we want our children to respect us, we must begin by respecting them, tiny as they may be. Here, right here, we begin to develop self-esteem.

Of all the abuses we heap on children, verbal abuse may be the most damaging, the most destructive, simply because it is so common, and generally not recognized for what it is, *abuse*. Victims of constant verbal abuse grow up with little or no self-esteem. They are often humiliated in public and made to feel that the rest of the world by inevitably keeping silent sides with the abuser.

Verbal abuse takes many forms. Consider the parent who does not call a child by name, but rather uses demeaning phrases such as "Hey, you!" or "You did it wrong again, Bozo," or "You are just as stupid as your stupid friends." How does a stupid child behave? Stupidly. The words we direct to a child form the fabric of which she is made. If she is beautiful she will grow up seeking constant confirmation of her beauty because she has been repeatedly told she is ugly. A smart child cannot develop her mind if her time is spent questioning her intelligence. Few children develop to their full potential under an onslaught of verbal abuse.

Who of us cannot recall the time when we strode into a grocery store and heard a mother savagely berate her child for misbehaviour? Every parent could cheerfully strangle her child while out on a shopping trip. "Put back the cornflakes, don't take the tomatoes from the bottom of the pyramid; no, you can't have the sugar-coated, toasty-woasty, marshmallow-dunked-yum-yum cereal, and if you ask one more time, you'll be sent to your room when we get home."

This is not verbal abuse. Verbal abuse is meant to harm. Its sources are dissatisfaction with our own lives and unresolved conflicts that stem from our childhood. As a result, we place unrealistic expectations on our children. One exasperated mother may say, "I swear, if you don't go to bed, I'll strangle

2

you", another one may scold, "You inconsiderate little brat, go to sleep." The one child will trudge off to bed knowing his fate is to sleep and dream while another has had judgment passed on his whole character.

What to do when talking to our children about misbehaviour? Avoid sentences that begin with "You are a . . . ." Remember that children are *never* bad, what they *do* might be bad, how they *act* might be bad, but they are not bad children. They are neither apples nor "veggies" or freezer foods. Children are NEVER BAD!

Then there is the parent who believes that the only way his child will succeed in the world is through constant "constructive" criticism. "If he doesn't get corrected at home, he surely will out there," is his rally cry. He uses this philosophy to demean the child's efforts, all under the auspicious excuse of preparing him for the hard realities of life. Only the very hardheaded survive such treatment. Most come to believe that if they don't get support on the home front, they most certainly won't get it out there in the jungle; and so they give up or perhaps give in.

There is another ugly form of hidden abuse — dogmatic one-line rules expressed to "protect children." "Don't talk to strangers" is one of them. Do we intend harm when we give our children such a rule? No, because it is said out of our fear, out of love and concern, in an attempt to simplify the entire confusing issue of protection. Our feelings often are, "She wouldn't understand, so I'll just give her this global rule." The trouble is, it will be applied to all situations.

One well may argue that this rule has been around forever and, frankly, it never did us much harm. It never did us much good either, however, something has been added; we are repeating it in a new and harsher way. We are screaming it loudly or whispering it dogmatically, reinforced with innuendoes and vague threats. ". . . If you talk to strangers, we will never see you again. You'll be taken away, you will never sleep in your own bed, never see your teddy bear, never . . . ever . . . ever."

Our children's sense of self — their self-esteem — is fundamental to their well-being. Their views of themselves and of their worth will influence all aspects of their lives.

Decision and Judgment Making

The second major characteristic of a streetproofed child is his ability to make decisions and pass judgments.

Even infants can make decisions. Yes they can! Ask an eight-months-old baby, "Which toy would you like to play with? This fuzzy, white, soft bunny or the big and noisy red rattle? See you can shake it . . ." Now, most self-respecting infants will want both, first the one and then the other. On the other hand, they might decide they don't want either. Normal. A two-year-old may decide which outfit she would like to wear today, given the choice of two equally suitable ones. A three-year-old can decide which street to take if he is familiar with the area. "Should we go down this street with the sidewalks or that one without sidewalks?"

What is of prime concern to a parent who offers options to a child? What if our three-year-old makes the wrong decision by choosing the street without the sidewalks? A child should never feel that he is wrong by not giving the preferred answer. "Oh, you want to go down the street without the sidewalks. Well, it is easier to ride your trike there, that is true and it is the fastest way home. But don't you think that riding/walking on the sidewalk is safer? After all, cars are bigger than us. They could knock us down. Ouch." All this talk takes time and practice. We are not used to really *talking* to children. It is easier to direct them onto the right path without explanation. But it is only easier in the short run.

Continually, we make decisions for our children that would be best left up to them. Many day care centres are the worst offenders by not allowing children to make decisions. Time is regimented and like little soldiers, children follow remote, unexplained schedules that must be kept. Naptime: 1:10; bathroom time: 2:15; heaven help the child who has to go at 1:10 and is sleepy at 2:15. In one day care centre I visited, a harassed worker doled out crayons, two at a time, to fifteen children. Ultimately, one child was the sad recipient of one purple and one black one. I suggested that perhaps all the crayons could be placed in an area where the children could pick the colours they wanted. (Better still, why not break the bank and buy fifteen boxes of crayons!) I was told that picking out their own would be too time consuming. There would hardly be any time left for colouring, and they would fight over them, too. "Besides," whispered the worker so that only ten of the fifteen children should hear, "a child's picture often reflects his inner thoughts, and it is important to see what goes on in his home environment." I wondered aloud what kind of picture the child with the black and purple crayon would draw and what dastardly conclusions this well-meaning teacher would come up with.

It may be said that by allowing children to select their own clothes, design their own rooms, choose what they would like to eat for lunch we are not initiating decision making at all. Rather, we are only giving children choices. If that is your belief, then stand with your child in front of a candy counter (a toy display, etc.) and ask her to choose one thing. Oh, the agony! She will peruse and dither, touch and examine, ponder and inspect, driving you crazy as the minutes tick by. This is an important decision in the making, perhaps the most important one of the week!

Before a child can make big decisions, he must experience making little ones. However, even little ones sometimes are overpowering. In Mary Susan Miller's excellent book, *Child Stress*, she states, "Too much freedom is as fearsome to a child as too little; it places on his shoulders more independence than he can handle. Haven't we all seen the three-year-old unable to decide what to choose for lunch, throw a tantrum and eat nothing? Similarly, haven't we seen the pre-adolescent filled with self-loathing over an act he committed? Excessive freedom creates guilt and self-doubt, and although growing up is synonymous with fighting to obtain that freedom, being granted it too soon is synonymous with unhappiness. That is a paradox of childhood: simultaneously striving for and turning away from independence. There is no winning."

Offering options is important to a streetproofed child. Not all children can cope with making these choices all the time. Likewise, a child may be capable of making the right decision one day and incapable of making the same one the next day. Balance is the key. If a child shows stress, backtrack, take matters gently but firmly into your own hands.

As a rule of thumb let children make only those choices and decisions that reflect on themselves. The responsibility of deciding for others is often too much to handle and the consequences or pain caused to others are too remote to deal with.

Don't offer choices with which you cannot live. For example, if you want Johnny to wear a particular outfit explain why you would like him to wear these clothes. Or, if Dad is in a hurry to get home do not ask your child to pick the longer way. Obvious statements. Sometimes we forget the obvious.

How do we help children make judgments? At first, ask them to judge such simple things as books. While reading to your child, find out what he thinks of the story. Did he enjoy it? Did he like the characters?

Little Red Riding Hood might well be the best streetproofing book ever written. Let me explain: First of all, she goes through the woods. Ask your child if Little Red Riding Hood's mother was right to send her there. Big people, even Mom's, can make mistakes. Was there a better way to Grandma's house? "Should Little Red Riding Hood have stopped to talk to the wolf? Would you? Besides, what business was it of the wolf where she was going and what was in her basket? He was too nosey. We don't have to answer nosey people's questions." Another reason why this may be an excellent streetproofing story is quite simply that a stranger (the wolf) gets the little girl into trouble; but look, another stranger (the woodcutter) gets her out of trouble! You may also want to add, "Do you think Little Red Riding Hood was a dumbbell?"

I made the mistake of reading this story to a seven-year-old who was way ahead of me. I asked him the above questions, finishing off with, "What do you think would have happened to Little Red Riding Hood if she had not talked to the wolf?" To which he replied, "The story wouldn't have been written and some guy wouldn't have made pots of money."

Judging the behaviour of book characters can be a good introduction to learning about people. Often, when a child passes judgment on adult behaviour, we scold her for being rude or insolent. Yet, children need to understand what constitutes acceptable behaviour, and the only way they can comprehend so difficult a concept is to allow them to make their own judgments.

In Linda Tschirhart Sandford's book, *The Silent Children*, she displays the different ways we label adult and child behaviour.

Behaviour	In a child it is called:	In an adult it is called:
Asking someone to blow his cigarette smoke in another direction	insolent	assertive
Not doing a job until the financial arrangements are clear	greediness	good business sense
Refusing to give up the chair he has been sitting in for an hour	selfishness	standing up for one's rights
Not eating everything on the dinner plate	picky eater	not hungry
Cutting in front of a line	pushy	in a hurry
Asking someone how much their new car cost	nosey	direct
Knocking something over and breaking it	clumsy	an accident
Striking a bargain: "I'll be glad to do this if you help me with . . ."	calculating	negotiating

Encouraging Instincts

The third characteristic of a streetproofed child is that he has learned to trust his instincts.

As a general rule and on principle, our society tends to frown on instincts. Heaven help the poor sod who says, "My instincts tell me . . ." What, no proof? No seven hundred-and-fifty-page study to back you up? No footnotes? No precedent? Many parents find themselves saying to their pediatrician, "I don't know what is wrong with my child. Something is, I can feel it." Too often, the reply is a patronizing pat on the back and a shoo out the door. "Just another over-anxious mother," is the unsaid connotation. How quickly we discount our own instincts relying instead on the authority of a battery of faceless statisticians. Happily, some people reach adulthood with their instincts intact, a little frayed at the edges perhaps, but preserved nonetheless. They become our leaders, our scientists, our explorers, and what drives them is belief in themselves and trust in their instincts.

How do we encourage children to develop their instincts? We can begin by *not* telling them that what *they* think and feel is subject to what *we* think and feel.

Have you heard this lately? "Go to bed. You are tired." What we mean is, "Go to bed, I'm tired."

How about this one? "No, you are not hungry. You just ate an hour ago." Have we never been hungry an hour after we have eaten?

Try this one. "I don't care if you are hot. Keep that sweater on, it's cold." I overheard another one in a library when a child, perhaps six years old, said, "I'm bored. I want to go outside." The mother's reply, "No you're not. You want to finish that book."

We must begin by recognizing that children are born with instincts. When we ignore their comments and feelings we are sabotaging their earliest alarm systems. They know what they feel, what they are capable of, what is right for them.

Here is yet another remark that harms not only a child's instincts, but becomes part and parcel of verbal abuse: "What's the matter with you, all the other kids in your class jumped into the deep end. These swimming lessons cost good money, and if you don't want to learn like everyone else, just say so." Chances are, had the child found a way to talk about his fears, sooner or later he would have attempted the great leap. As it stands, if he does jump into the pool the next time, he will do it not because of his own desire but to gain parental approval. On the other hand, he may dig in his heels and develop a long-term dislike of water. Either way, everyone loses.

Pushing a child into great and wonderful ventures has become a pastime for the modern mother. "What, your child is not in a Montessori school? Why you . . . you . . . bad mother you!" "You mean to tell me your Doug is not taking Susuki classes? Don't you want him to love music?" Certainly, providing new experiences is a pleasure no parent or child should miss but the occupation should suit both. A mother wanted her daughter to learn to play the violin. "I wish I liked violin music," she said. "Actually, I hate it." Learning should be fun.

Fun is not a dirty word. Learning about streetproofing can be fun. Yes, raising children is serious business, but it is so much fun!

Discussing Sex with Small Children

Children need to know about sex and sexuality. For generations the topic was clouded and shrouded in veils of mystery. Inadvertently, it was made exciting and, at the same time, incredibly confusing. Why? Because that is how sex was taught (or not taught) to us. We learned through intimation, nuance and, in the end, by osmosis!

It was decided that sex is for big people, all the while acknowledging that yes, children are being sexually abused at an alarming rate. To not talk to young children about sex because it embarrasses us is to suggest that our feelings are more important than their well-being.

Another reaction to the idea of talking to very young children about sex is that it "takes away their childhood" or will produce a "hurried child." Parents with unrealistic expectations produce hurried children. Teaching about sex will no more take away childhood than letting a kid watch the birth of a kitten. It is part of his world and he has a right to know about it.

Most of us wait to discuss sex until we think the child is of "proper age." One stout-hearted and determined mother told me that she intended to speak to her son about sex one month before he reached puberty! We may be waiting for that magical day when we are at peace with the world. When the bills have been paid, dinner has been prepared, all household tasks have been completed. In will bound our beautiful twelve-year-old with the question, "Mommy, where do babies come from?" And in the soft shimmering light of sunset, we will speak of procreation. . . . Hang on, that day will never come. My own mother still is waiting for it!

Children ask us about sex or sexually related subjects all the time. It is our choice to interpret their questions. Here are some examples:

"How come Bobby gets to wear a little bathing suit, and I have to wear a great big one?"

"How come Daddy can cut the grass without a shirt and you can't?"

9

"What are these?" (Holding up tampons while you are entertaining dinner guests).

How do we talk to small children about sex? Where do we begin? It would be easier to forget about it, to say to ourselves, "He is too young," or "When she is ready, she will ask. I don't want to put ideas into her head."

Example:

Billy is six years old. One moment he is sweet, adorable, disarming but the next he is a demon on two feet, swatting his baby sister, watering the rug, and zooming down the bannister at breakneck speed.

Billy has always come to us with questions: "How come people on the other side of the earth don't fall off?" "How do all those people fit into our T.V. set?" And somehow we answer him. One day, Billy says, "Mom, what does 'fuck you' mean?" We fall into a dead faint, send him to his room, lock the door and don't want to let him out until he is 36. Why? What has Billy learned by our actions? That there are some things about which kids do not talk to parents, and others that are to be kept secret from big people. Is Billy likely to forget the question? No, but he will look to another source for the answer. Maybe he will ask Jimmy down the street? Jimmy is seven and worldly; he will know.

Chances are that Billy knew this was a "special" question. He probably had heard the phrase used as an insult, perhaps even one cast in his direction. Maybe he wanted to see what Mom would do and he did not care what she said?

What reply can we give Billy? Here are some suggestions:

"Billy, that is a good question, and I would like to answer it. Give me a minute and I'll be right with you." (If you need time).

or

"Where did you hear that, Billy?"

and

"It means when a man puts his penis in a woman's vagina. We call that making love and it is a nice thing to do for two grown people who love each other. It is also how a baby is made. Most people consider the words, 'fuck you' to be insulting. They offend people. Please do not use these words outside the house and inside as little as possible." (You may want to add, and never in front of your grandmother!)

This conversation will, in all likelihood, go right over Billy's head. Body language and tone of voice are much more important at this stage than the related information. The point is that Billy knows he can ask questions. He also knows that if a question is asked in good faith he will get an answer.

Example:

Erika is the proud mother of three children. Both she and husband Peter decided to be open with and approachable to their children. One spring day, Erika felt it was time for five-year-old Christopher to learn about sexuality. So she said to him, "Chris, I want to tell you what sex is. Are you listening? Well, sex is when a man puts his penis into a woman's vagina. We call that making love."

Christopher did not seem overly thrilled with this revelation, so Erika decided not to further pursue the matter. She would try again another day.

That night, while watching his father shave in preparation for an evening out, Christopher decided to show off his newly found knowledge. "Dad, I know what Texas is," he said. Peter continuing his shave asked, "What?" "Tex-as" (or, sex is) replied Christopher, "is when a man puts his penis in Regina." Needless to say, Peter had a very close shave!

Children do hear what we say. They may not always quite understand, but most will come to comprehend by the age of twelve the entire conception and birth process. This is not to say that we cannot begin to discuss sex earlier adding information as the child and the questions prosper.

Give your child a chance to display what she knows. Ask her to tell another adult about what she has learned. Do not interrupt, judge or correct. Let her have her moment in the sun; there is time to sort out things later, when you and she are alone again.

Children do seek out the information they need. Where do they get it? According to Irving R. Dickman, author of *Winning the Battle for Sex Education* (Siecus Publications, New York, N.Y., 1982):

37 % from peers
22 % from media
17.4% from mothers
15.2% from schools
.5% from ministers
.3% from physicians

In short, a whopping 82.5% of all children learn about sex outside the home!

We cannot change our children's overall environment. However, we have the power to talk to them about sexuality, love, and intimacy. Define these words for yourself. What do they mean? When talking to your child about sex include your own feelings and thoughts. You can do it.

Howard and Martha Lewis, in their book, *Sex Education Begins at Home*, discuss "doctor" play in realistic, healthy terms. "The urge towards sex games seems almost as common among children as the impulse to play tag. Your youngster may meet another child in the park. Five minutes after seeing each other, they may be behind a bush with their clothes off. Such sex play may involve children of the same sex or the opposite sex. For most children, it is an occasional occurrence and seems to diminish as the child approaches puberty."

In most cases, such play represents the child's healthy curiosity about his own body and the bodies of others. Even in older children, perhaps aged 8 to 11, sexual games are unlikely to lead to attempted intercourse.

Most of us remember playing doctor in the garage, the basement, or other out-of-the-way place. The mere fact that children tend to carry on their investigations in secrecy, suggests that while they know this is interesting stuff, they also realize there is something not quite socially acceptable about it. What do we do when we discover our child playing doctor with a neighbour's child? Do we indignantly march in anddemand that they stop? Do we call up our neighbour and suggest she take her deviant child to a psychiatrist? Surely, hers must have persuaded mine to behave in this way! By taking this approach we are only telling our children that they are wrong. Consequently, sex is wrong.

The Lewis' suggest that such games be interrupted by saying gently but firmly, "Time to put your clothes on now." Richard M. Sarles of the University of Maryland School of Medicine in Baltimore further recommends that you do not dismiss such incidents but discuss them openly. "Mommy and Daddy know that children like to play doctor because they want to know what boys and girls look like or wonder where babies come from." This non-punitive approach has countless benefits toward an open, healthy discussion about sex, as well as lending itself to easy communication — a key point for the street-proofed child.

According to Sarles, "In general, you need to worry about your children's sex play only if it seems to be their favourite activity. A youngster who frequently engages in sex games may be over-stimulated by an adult, or may have an emotional problem." He also cautions parents to be concerned if the play is marked by aggressive or sadistic behaviour, "such as forced heterosexual or homosexual contact."

If two or more children are playing "operations," a parent need not be concerned if they are within one age group e.g. not more than three years apart. Concern is justified when one child is five and the other one ten, simply because the older one will be better informed and, therefore, dominate the procedure.

Children who have *not* received guidance also experiment. However, we are more likely to get a recounting of exploits from whose who are well informed.

When talking to children about sex we must include discussion of the sharing and caring. To only deal with the technical aspects of love-making is to confuse and, ultimately, short change the child. Above all, look at the entire subject with respect and good humour.

A high sense of self-worth, the ability to make decisions and judgments, good instincts, a sound knowledge of sex, and the feeling of being loved, make up a streetproofed child. But is ᵗreetproofing the reason why we encourage these qualities? Of course not. We value our children because they are who they are. We want them to be happy and healthy and, in the end, they will be better protected because of our good parenting.

13

II

THE RULES

Somewhere along the line you may be thinking, yes, all this encouragement of self-esteem, ability to make decisions and judgments, and talking about sex is fine, but what about streetproofing? What about the rules? We are all familiar with them, good grief, we can't pick up a magazine, a newspaper, or turn on the radio without the rules glaring or blaring at us. Ten years ago, discussion of sexual abuse was non-existent. No one in their right mind wanted to talk about it. Five years ago, one could not utter the word incest in polite company. Now the topic is dished out at cocktail parties along with the canapés.

Streetproofing is another topic of the day. "Say, Martha, is your Susie streetproofed yet?" or, "By the way, Alison, how did you explain rape to your Billy?"

Most media people seem to feel that the way to a parent's heart is through shock treatment. Predominantly, the rules can be found in magazine articles, boxed for easy reference. They usually lead off with a horror story with the overriding theme, "This could happen to your child if you don't teach him the rules."

Applying the Rules

Dogmatic one-liners seldom, if ever, work. Chances are children will apply one of three tactics when handed down such rules.

1. The child may take the rule and apply it to one specific occasion only. All rules must be part and parcel of a conversation.

Rule:

"Don't get into a car with anyone unless I know about it first."

Application:

"I told my six-year-old not to get into cars with strangers. I mean, that is a sensible rule, isn't it? How was I to know he would get onto the back of a motorcycle? What should I have said, 'Don't get into any cars, motorcycles, planes, trains or ships?' "

2. The child may take the rule and apply it to all occasions.

Rule:
"Don't get on an elevator unless there are at least two people in it."

Application:
"There was a flasher in our apartment building. All the kids knew who he was, but few of the adults did.

"We were all really worried and so we called a meeting with children and parents. One woman got up and told the children not to get into elevators unless there were two adults present. The children repeated that rule over and over again. Later, some mothers told me that their youngsters were frightened of the elevator. One mother had to walk up twelve flights with her four-year-old because he wouldn't set foot in it.

"Anyway, about a week later, my ten-year-old daughter got into the elevator with the flasher and his friend. Can you believe that? I mean, she knew this guy! She was one of the children who had been flashed! When I asked her how she could be so stupid, she just shrugged and said, 'I wanted to get home. Besides, there was another guy in the elevator.' "

3. By applying the rule the child may put his/her life at risk.

Rule:
"Take care of that bike. It is your responsibility to see that it does not get damaged or stolen."

Application:
"When we gave our son a two-wheeler for his eighth birthday his father told him to take good care of it. Well, maybe he did overdo it . . . I saw that car coming down the street and Matthew standing there with his bike in the middle of the road. I thought the world would cave in. Instead of getting out of the way, he tried to save the bike. Thank God, the car swerved."

The rules can be confusing. Perhaps there are so many that the child cannot make sense of all of them and, therefore, dismisses them altogether. Picture Abby, a six-year-old, on the way out to play. "Mom", she calls from the doorway, "I'm going over to Jason's house, see ya." It is not that easy, Abby. Before you can get out the door, you must listen to the rules:

Don't go with strangers.

Don't talk to strangers. If you see a stranger and he talks to you, run.

Look both ways before you cross the street. Cross at the corner.

Do not lose that new sweater.

Don't go anywhere with anyone unless I know about it.

Don't climb trees.

Don't hang upside down on the monkey bars with a dress on.

Don't cut across Mr. Smith's backyard.

Don't leave your bike on the driveway.

Stay away from the big kids.

Don't touch any wires.

Don't throw stones.

Don't . . . Don't . . . Don't . . ."

Is Abby going to go out and have a good time? She might because chances are she has dismissed everything Mom has told her. Is Mom about to enjoy an hour of leisure? Perhaps, but only if she believes that Abby has heard and understood every word she said.

Children need rules. They need to know the boundaries of commonsense and of acceptable behaviour. Explain to them that it is important to keep track of their possessions but emphasize that nothing, absolutely nothing, is more important than their safety.

We, the adults, also must follow the rules if we want our children to respect them. How often do we demand of a child, "I want to know where you are and with whom," and then pop out to the store without informing any one.

Rules that Work

Checking in:

Example A:

"David, it is important that your Mom and I know where you are at all times. It also is important that you know where your Mom and I are at all times. That means, we do not want you to go anywhere with anyone unless you ask us or your baby-sitter first.

"Let's say you are at a friend's house and his Dad says, 'Everyone in the car, we are going out for ice-cream.' What would you do? I'll bet it would be really hard to say, 'I can't go unless I call my parents.' but that's the rule: IF YOU CANNOT CHECK, YOU CANNOT GO."

Example B:

Parent: "Let's say someone you know — a teacher or a neighbour — came up to you and asked you to come with them for a hamburger or to see a litter of kittens. What would you say"?

Child: "First, I'd tell them that I had to ask my Mom."

Parent: "What would you say if they said, 'I just spoke with your Mom on the phone. She says it's alright.' Now, what would you say?"

Child: "I still have to call my Mom."

Parent: "We don't want you to go anywhere with anyone unless we know about it first."

What if the child comes up with the wrong answer?

Parent: "What would you do if someone you know well asked you to go with them?"

Child: "I would go, I guess."

Parent: "I can understand why you might feel this way, but think about the rule: 'Check first.' "

Child: "You mean, I still have to call you, even if I know the person well?"

Parent: "Right. THAT IS THE RULE."

Watch when crossing the street:

Do you tell your child to look both ways every time you cross a street with him? The answer is "Yes." Even toddlers in strollers can be taught to look both ways. How often do we see a mother pushing a carriage along a street, her back to the traffic? Another common sight is a parent slowly pushing out a carriage between parked cars, and only then looking both ways to see if traffic is coming.

Other rules:

In addition, there are the rules that pertain just to your own circumstances. For example, a family who lives near the water might have special water rules, and people who live near train tracks would, no doubt, have rules that apply specifically to trains.

The suggestion here is that we take a good, hard look at all the rules we've got and decide which ones are of primary importance. Think about them, look at them from every possible angle. If you find there are more exceptions than constants, change the rules.

We want to give children guidelines with which we all can live for a long time. Naturally, the old household rules still apply, such as "Don't put anything but a plug into electrical outlets." "Why?" "Because you can get an electric shock, ouch!" Small children do not know what electricity is and yet, most find this to be an acceptable answer and, with regular reminders, will stay clear of electric sockets. Even if we have given a child a rule about electricity and an explanation of the rule, do we remove the safety caps that cover the outlets? No, because children often regress, forget, or succumb to their curiosity. Apply that same reasoning to streetproofing. Assume that children forget, no matter how often your repeat the rules.

Sometimes Bad Things Happen to Good People

We lead children to believe that goodness will bring success, love, accomplishment. If you are good, then the world will be good to you. If you follow the rules, nothing bad will happen.

How can we make children understand that even if we follow the rules, do our best to protect ourselves, sometimes things can go wrong?

Example:

"Andrea, sometimes bad things happen to good people, did you know that? Can you think of something bad that happened to someone you love? . . . Aunt Dorothy broke her leg. Yes, that is a good example. It wasn't Aunt Dorothy's fault that she hurt herself . . . Cousin Sue had a car accident, that's another good example.

"Both Aunt Dorothy and Aunt Susan had bad things happen to them and yet, they are both nice people. What if somebody made you feel bad or tricked you into doing something that was not right? Who's fault would it be?"

Sometimes good people or people we perceive to be good, do bad things. Ask your child if she can think of a bad thing a good person did. Expect this sort of reply, "You mean like the time Uncle Ralph got into a fight with Uncle Robert and hit him?" Admitting that we too sometimes lose control will help a child understand that good people can do bad things.

III

LOST AND FOUND

If you have ever been lost as a child or been separated from your Mom and Dad while out shopping, you will never forget the acute feelings of helplessness and vulnerability. I recently spoke with a gentle, dewy-eyed eighty-eight-year-old woman. She was unsure of the last meal she had eaten and yet she spoke with clarity and conviction of her childhood:

> "I remember being lost as a child. It was just before the end of the war, the Great War of course. We lived just outside of London then. One day my Mother took me with her into the city. It was such a great event. My Mother's youngest brother was in hospital there, you see. We landed in the train station. Such a big place, so big, so grand. The ceiling went up to heaven. People were everywhere, pushing and shoving. I had never seen so many people. Uniforms were everywhere too. Those men didn't look like soldiers to me, not at all. They looked just like boys. And then I got lost. My mother wasn't in front of me anymore. I called out to her, but there was so much noise. A man in a blue coat came up to me and asked me if I was lost. He looked like such a funny man. He had on a fur collar. I'd never seen such a man. I wasn't supposed to talk to strangers, so I ran away. A soldier helped me. He took me to the ticket wicket and they sat me up there like an ornament. I sat and sat. Lots of people asked me my name, but I wouldn't tell them. I was too scared."

Getting lost or losing a child in a public place are problems that have been around since time began. While we usually do our best to see that our children do not stray, we must take positive action to minimize the risk and ease a child's stress should such an event take place.

First, let us look at several different ways children react when they are lost:

a) The Runners: When these children find they have been separated from Mom and Dad they begin to run.

b) The Criers: These children remain standing in one spot and begin to sob or wail. The volume of tears and noise level increase when they are offered help.

c) The Hiders: In department stores these children may be found among long dresses or coats, under shelving units or crouched low in corners.

d) The Wanderers: They usually are fairly confident children; if they cannot be found in a relatively short period of time, they often assume any one of the above behaviour patterns.

Lost in a Shopping Mall

Given the habits of today's society, most children will, at times, find themselves separated from their parents in shopping centres. If that is a likelihood in your family, talk about this eventuality while you are inside the shopping mall. It is useless to sit a child down in the kitchen and ask him to picture the layout of your local complex. Begin the conversation as you enter it and continue in stops and starts until your shopping expedition is completed. It might be possible to spend a day out pursuing this project.

When you are in the shopping centre, kneel down to your child's eye level and look around. The place sure seems different from this vantage point, doesn't it? Then ask your child, "If you and I were separated (don't say lost) right here, who would you go to for help?" Now, if you have told your child not to talk to strangers, you may be in a quandary. At this point, mention the best people for her to approach. Remember, we want her to ask for help, not stand still and receive it. Here is a list of people you may point out to your child:

1. Mothers with small children: They can be found in large numbers in most shopping centres. Mothers will help. They also become extraordinarily protective about other people's lost children. They tend to stay with the child, surrendering him only to the parent.

2. Store personnel: Point out to your child cashiers and

cash areas, ID buttons, and if applicable, smocks or uniforms of store personnel.

3. Grannies: Older women are a good resource and least likely to harm a child.

4. Police officers: I think they are an excellent resource but, frankly, are seldom around when they are needed. When was the last time you saw a police officer wandering around a shopping mall?

There is a second reason why I don't recommend that *small* children seek out the police for help. Under seven they rarely can differentiate between a police uniform and any other uniform. If you doubt this, ask your five-year-old during an excursion to point out every police person he can see. Make the game interesting and say, "Every time you correctly identify a police officer, I will give you a nickel." You may find that doormen, limousine drivers, porters, men with crests on their jackets, even men with hats on also will qualify!

Police officers who are not busy are usually happy to show children their badges and identifications.

The bogey man and the policeman are not interchangeable characters. Avoid the statement, "If you are bad, the police will take you away and put you in jail." A child is not likely to ask for help from a person who might do that to him.

The police are not our "friends." They are a resource because they maintain the law. We do not say to a child, "Your teacher or the lifeguard is your friend." And yet, these people are there to help us. Friends come to our house for dinner; we share confidences with them; they are people we love and trust.

Lost at a Fair

The idea of losing a child at a sports arena, in a circus tent, or at an exhibition rings terror in the hearts of parents. What can we do before such an outing begins?

- Put v ery small children in a harness.
- Older children should be taken to a designated meeting place and told specifically, "This is where we meet if we are separated."
- Children too old to be in a harness and too young to find a meeting place must be told to seek help from a mother with small children. Again, the premise is: We want our

children to be the initiators. We want *them* to ask for help.

Suggestions have been made to establish Block Parent booths in and around fairgrounds. This is a wonderful idea. If you are a member of such an organization or a similar volunteer group and you know that an exhibition is coming to your area, suggest the idea at the next meeting. If it meets with everyone's approval, take the initiative to implement it. All you need is a few willing people, preferably those who have given permission to have their credentials checked out by the police, one or more booths, a sign that will attract children, and flyers to promote the program.

As the prevalence of abductions comes to light, more and more entertainment companies will be willing to cooperate.

Lost on a City Street

Discuss with your child what positive action can be taken if you are separated from each other on the street.

Suggestions:

1. "Stop. Take a good look around but don't cross any streets."

2. "If you can't see me, go directly into a store and ask the person behind the counter to please call the police. I would rather you not accept anyone's help. If someone offered to help you, what would you say?"

3. "See those people handing out parking tickets? You could go to one of them if you saw one. However, I do not want you to go looking for one."

4. Taxi drivers are another resource for children alone on a city street, particularly after shopping hours. The old rule applies, of course, "Do not go anywhere with anyone. Do not get into the cab."

Taxi drivers have radios and can call the police. Once the child has informed the driver and asked for help, he should stand back and wait . . . Yes, I know, it is not a great tactic, but we are trying to do the best we can.

Lost on Public Transit

Increasingly, children under ten are using buses, streetcars, and subways. Except for their size, it is sometimes hard to single them out from the rest of the commuting world. Before you yourself take your child on a public transit system or if he goes on his own, spend some time talking about it.

In the subway children should sit in the first car close to the driver. Show your child the emergency cord and how it works. It is unfortunate that the emergency buttons are placed too high for most children to reach.

How many parents have not envisioned standing on a subway platform, watching the doors close? Child is in the car, parent outside, or vice versa. If you are inside the car, hit the emergency button. If you are on the platform, move. There usually are five to 15 minutes between trains. Inform the authorities. Ask them to radio ahead to the next station and/or the subway driver. They are supposed to be prepared for such events.

Tell your child that if the door closes and you are split up, she is to hit the emergency button or ask the driver to do it for her. She also should get off at the next stop and wait. You will be on the next train. Ask her not to talk to anyone unless the person is wearing a subway system uniform.

Lost in the Suburbs

Many of us are living in homes or townhouses that closely resemble one another. If your house is not distinguishable from your neighbours', place something on the outside to make it identifiable at a glance. A brightly coloured flag or a piece of paper tacked to the door is all you really need, providing it cannot be swept away by the wind.

Then take lots of walks with your child around the area, pointing out the street signs. Explain the difference between a crescent, an avenue, a street, or a cul-de-sac. Point out homes with certain characteristics; laugh a little along the way. You can also count the Block Parent signs you see. Enjoy yourself by noticing the world from your child's height. Now look up and talk about the high wires and electricity. "See the trees? That one touches those wires. It would not be a good idea to climb that tree." What else do you see? The sewers. Talk about them.

Is there a ravine in your area? How about vacant or new homes? Many people who are used to taking a specific route home haven't the faintest idea of what's around their own community.

On the street, talk about all sorts of dangers. Play the "What If" game. (Chapter XVI) Discuss cars and crosswalks. Let your child give you advice; let her correct you. "Oh, Daddy, you didn't look both ways." Do not lead. Become part of a team and act as a team member.

Perhaps you want to find out where your child plays. What short-cuts does he use? It is best not to criticize his choice of play areas. If he takes you to the back of a store and shows you all the neat treasures that can be found in the garbage, don't show your distress because there is a good chance he won't show you how easy it is to walk, eyes closed, across the cement ledge by the reservoir.

Listen to your child, hear what he is saying:

"If I walk like this, I can step on all those wood things on the railway tracks." Wood things? Railway tracks?

"The backstairs at Jimmy's apartment building wobble. They are neat." Backstairs? Wobble? Who is Jimmy?

On walks with your child you have, no doubt, pointed out and explained all about Block Parents. You have told him about the police and what they do. Naturally, you always walk facing the traffic — yes, even on sidewalks. Perhaps you have discussed what children should do when they are approached for directions from a car: "Stand back on the grass and say you don't know. Leave the scene in the opposite direction the car has been travelling."

You and your child have come a long way in streetproofing, and all you have done is go for a walk. Congratulations!

Lost Child — the Parent's Role

"What would you do if you lost your child in a shopping mall?" Over the years, I have put this question to hundreds of parents and always received the one and only initial response: "Panic." Many parents say this to me with a smile on their

faces, the connotation being, "We wouldn't panic, not really."
But they do and behave just the way they tell their children not
to behave. Alright, you have lost your child in the shopping centre. Look around and allow yourself two-and-a-half seconds of
panic. That's enough time wasted. Now what do you do?

1. Call out. Open your mouth and call out his or her name.
Remember, we have told children that it is OK to be loud in
public when there is a good reason. This is a good reason for
you to be loud!

2. Approach a cashier. Most stores will take positive action
but occasionally you will come across an uncooperative clerk.
One mother was told to go to the "Lost and Found" and wait!
Be assertive, be aggressive, be whatever you have to be to get
immediate attention. However, this is still not enough.

3. Ask for help from every mother you see. This may be
embarrassing but remember, that embarrassment is part and
parcel of parenthood. Some of us have difficulty asking for
help: we are supposed to be self-reliant and independent. When
we need help our child's safety takes precedent over everything
else in the world. Open your mouth and speak: "Excuse me, I
can't find my daughter. She is four. She has black hair and is
wearing a pink outfit with a rabbit on the front. Please stand by
that door." — "Excuse me, my daughter is four. I can't find
her. She . . ." Go. Run. Keep talking. I've seen this plan in
action and it works. No one will think any less of you, I pro-
mise. No one will judge you. We are all in this world together.
Every parent knows that the child they are looking for could be
their own.

Having driven an entire store into action by summoning
help from every possible source, you may find Mary happily
playing with the tags of some dresses. What to do? Shoot her?
That is one way to avoid a repeat incident. What the heck, give
her a hug! It will do you both the world of good.

Home Fires Burning

While the topic of house fires does not come under streetproofing proper, a suggestion about it is not entirely out of
place here. Every year, in every schoolroom across the nation,
children are trained to line up, lock the windows and proceed
calmly out the door at the sound of a fire alarm. School fire in-

cidents are minimal, but children need to know how to behave and how to escape from a home fire. Here is what one mother had to say:

"We decided to have a home fire drill. My husband and I talked to the children beforehand about such things as touching a door before opening it to see if it is hot. We discussed how to crawl under the smoke, not to look for us, just to get out. One evening, just before bed, we set off the fire detector in our home. Nothing happened. My three kids continued watching TV. Finally, I trudged up to the TV room and asked them if they were deaf. Their reply, 'We thought it was just another false alarm.' Well, we explained in no uncertain terms that whenever they hear the alarm, they must react.

"We tried again a week later. Two of my three children instantly left what they were doing and went outside. My husband found our six-year-old daughter crying in her bedroom on the main floor. She said she couldn't get the window open. It struck me that in a real fire, she still would not have broken it. We have taught our children to respect possessions. We had to calmly sit down with all of them and say plainly, 'You have the right to protect yourselves even if you have to break a window to do it. Throw a chair through the window. Nothing is more important than your safety."

The Safe Arrival Program

What if . . . your child left for school at 8:35 a.m. and never arrived there. Perhaps she decided to play hooky, perhaps she was hurt, perhaps she was abducted. Chances are you will not know about it until it is time for her to return home from school. If the search only begins at 4:30 p.m., then she has, in effect, been missing for eight hours! The key ingredient to finding a missing child is to act quickly. Eight hours is a long waiting time before the search begins.

A Safe Arrival Program (S.A.P.) can be implemented in any school, at any time. This is how it works. If a child will not attend school on a given day, Mom or Dad must phone the school and report it. If the person answering the school phone does not recognize Mom's voice, she calls back to confirm.

The teacher takes attendance in the classroom, and then sends the list to the office. All names must be accounted for, either on the class list or on the phone-in list. Parents of a child whose name does not appear on either list receive a phone call. Simple.

As with any program, there always are a few exceptions that cause problems.

Example:

"I received a call at work from the school at 10:00. My seven-year-old son was not there. He had left for school at 8:45. 'Oh, God,' that's all I kept saying, 'Oh, God' and 'Please, God.' I left work and drove to the school in record time. I don't remember the drive nor parking the car. It's all a complete blank. I rushed into the school office and braced myself against a desk. My son was fine, they told me. He had been in the washroom during attendance. I flopped in a chair and sat there for twenty minutes."

Let's turn this experience around. No doubt this Mom had a bad scare and the school could have double checked before calling her. However, the system did work.

S.A.P. programs usually originate with the P.T.A. but must be implemented by all parents. You may be requested to volunteer one morning or less, per month. If you are a two-parent family, this will mean one morning per person every two months.

Some P.T.A.'s may have a campaign to raise funds for the program, proceeds to be used to hire a college student or parent every morning for one hour.

A Missing Child

If you have been informed that your child did not arrive at school . . .

- Ask the school to double check and then call the police.
- If you are separated from your spouse, give him or her a call and find out where he/she is or was. While non-custodial abduction may be a concern, it is also the other parent's perogative to know what is going on.

- Are there any other children missing from school? Is there a chance of a mini-exodus for the day? Is the weather nice? Most children will not play hooky during a snowstorm.
- Call up the parents of other children who have not been accounted for. If the children are friends, it will be easy to track them down by working together. Ask yourself, "Where is my child likely to be? Where is she not likely to be?"
- If you don't have a "calls waiting" system on your phone, stay off it. Your child may be trying to get through to you. Suggestion: Once a year or every six months, if you are very organized, sit down and write out all the names and phone numbers of your child's friends. Photocopy this list and give it to your best friend, preferably a stay-at-home Mom. If the situation warrants, call up that person and let her do the search by phoning all the numbers on the list. *Your line must be kept open.*

- While you will want to leave the house immediately, do not leave it empty. Find someone to sit in your home.
- Before you go out, check your own home. Look in the garage, in the attic.
- Check the child's room. Is there anything missing? Is the piggy bank full? Has your own wallet been pilfered? If nothing is missing, you can usually rule out a runaway.
- Has there been stress in your child's life lately? Has she been behaving normally over the past few days? Talk to your child's teacher.
- Generally speaking, the younger the child, the faster you must act.
- If the home front has been covered, you may want to move the search to the school. Phone numbers and telephone lines are more accessible there.
- Bring several copies of your child's photo with you.
- Start the search. While it would be difficult to justify a full-fledged effort at this point, remember that we are talking about small children, not teenagers. If you *feel* that something is amiss, act on it.
- Call up your friends. Get them to use their imagination and to assist you with such mundane things as having the

coffee pot full to keep up the search party's spirits. Your friends can provide valuable aid and support.

- Volunteers can be drawn from many sources. Start with your school's P.T.A. Call in service clubs; phone all the radio stations in your area. Have your child's picture delivered to any television station or newspaper that will accept it.
- Is there an organization in your area that can aid in your search, such as Child Find, etc.? Call them.
- Contact a citizen band radio. Give the operator accurate information. The idea is to get as many eyes as possible looking for your child.
- Taxi drivers also have radios. Call the dispatcher and give a description of your child.
- A foot patrol is usually undertaken by the police. If this has not been done, organize it yourself. Post a map on a board.
- The faster you move, the less time you will have to panic. If you appear scatterbrained and out of control, authorities may not be as helpful as they could be. Remember, panic clouds the mind. You will need all of your faculties.
- Do not be surprised if the police investigates friends, relatives, past boyfriends, etc. While such investigations might ruffle feathers, those who have a vested interest in finding your child will understand. A parent should provide all the necessary information, and more. Do not interfere with this part of the police's duty.

Most parents have the organizational abilities of multinational corporation executives. Remember that. However, if you cannot cope, find someone who can, preferably a person who also knows the area.

At this very moment, try to think what you would do if your child went missing. No, don't shudder and avoid the thought. Pour yourself a glass of wine or a cup of coffee and sit back. If you live in a rural community you likely will concentrate on organizing patrols. In an urban setting, focusing on the media might be more productive.

The next two pages have been left blank. Before you write in *your* contingency plan, talk to your spouse or a friend. Come on, you can do it!

Contingency Plan for Locating a Missing Child

Contingency Plan for
Locating a Missing Child

IV

A WORD ABOUT HANDICAPPED CHILDREN

The ideas suggested in the next three chapters are equally suitable for handicapped or disabled children. While their problems are unique in themselves, they are not always unique to their disability.

The Seattle Rape Relief Developmental Disabilities Project estimates that up to five hundred disabled children are abused each year in the Seattle area alone. A full 99 per cent of these victims are abused by a caretaker or by someone well known to the child and the family. It appears that a mere 20 per cent of offenses are reported.

Disabled children, like all children, are at risk. It is wrong to assume that a disability somehow protects, and that children with handicaps may be less vulnerable than normal ones.

The urge to molest stems not from sexual desire, but rather from the abuser's need to dominate and control. The degree of a child's disability determines the extent to which he/she is dependent on his/her caretaker. Children who must rely totally on adults for their physical as well as emotional needs, lack the information base from which to judge the behaviour of others. They are encouraged to be complacent and accepting, usually are without peer groups, and may not have the ability to communicate easily with others. For all the above reasons, they may prove to be *more* desirable to a potential offender.

Therefore, extra concern should be placed on discussing sex and sexuality with the handicapped. It is well known that many children pick up their knowledge of sex from the world around them. Hearing–impaired and blind children often miss out on this learning process. Sighted children have the advantage of seeing parents hug, show affection, pass loving glances.

Television also provides them with valuable insights. All of this is lost to the blind.

Privacy and developing personal space might be difficult for them to understand, just as children who require constant or repeated medical intervention might never realize the difference between needed treatment and abusive touching, unless they have been specifically told that their bodies belong to them, and they may reject unwanted advances.

Discuss with the child the necessary treatments. Respect his or her space and do not sit uninvited on a bedridden child's bed; refrain from physically manoeuvring him or her into different positions without his or her consent or knowledge.

Scan the next few chapters of this book with pen in hand, circling suggestions that are applicable to you and your special child.

V

CREATIVE STREETPROOFING FROM BIRTH TO THREE

The years between birth and three are precious. It is a time to learn trust and love, feel acceptance, and develop self-respect and confidence. To suggest that a baby or toddler could become streetproofed would be misleading, however, the foundations for it can and should be laid at that age.

Children develop at a pace unique unto themselves. Some of the streetproofing suggestions in this segment can be applied to four- and five-year-olds and, of course, vice versa.

The streetproofing ideas are gentle, creative, broad and accessible. Whether you are a parent, a grandparent, teacher, aunt, uncle or friend, you may also wish to develop some of your own ideas.

Body Awareness

It must strike children as odd that there are names for everything except that which exists between the navel and the knees! If we are going to teach them that their bodies belong to them, that the body is a beautiful and wonderful thing and that no one has the right to touch it in an abusive or unpleasant way, then we also must acknowledge their right to know the proper names for its parts.

Teaching these names is easy. When we say to our infant, "Look, here are your toes, see your toes?" we also can say, "This is your vulva, down here between your legs is the vulva."

Giving the private parts anatomically correct names tells a child that there is nothing wrong with these particular parts of the body. Nevertheless, no matter how forthright parents may be in stating these names, sooner or later, their children will discover that they are special words. A bright child will ask at dinner, "I have a penis, do you?" and Aunt Tildy will fall into her soup while Grandpa has cardiac arrest on the rug. Stay calm. If this truly bothers you, it is fair to say to the child that just as these are names for our private parts, so are the words that describe them private. On the other hand, if the use of these words does not bother you, then forget about mentioning anything.

Another excellent reason for teaching a child the proper names for body parts is to save teachers, day care workers and police officers, the time they often must spend decoding a child's nicknames for these body parts and their related functions.

Examples:

"I felt really sorry for the little kid. He wet his pants and was so embarrassed that he sat in a corner for the entire day. About an hour before he had said to me, "Can I squirt?" I was too preoccupied to understand and said, "Not now."

"His day care worker brought him to the nursing office around 1:00. He kept saying his elbow hurt. We examined it but were baffled. It was obvious he was in pain. Half an hour later, we asked him to point to where it hurt. He still pointed to his elbow. It turned out that he had fallen from the school monkey bars and had hurt his testicles. He was all crunched up, holding his arm over his pelvis. His elbow for which he knew the name, was the thing nearest to the pain."

"As police officers we were investigating an alleged molestation. A six-year-old girl sat before us. She appeared composed and rather articulate. The molestation by a relative had involved touching. One of the first questions we asked was, 'Where did he touch you?' She responded, 'On my powder puff.' Now I ask you?"

If you insist upon using nicknames, make sure you occasionally relate them to the real names for certain parts of the body.

A Creative Suggestion

To encourage body awareness, place a large piece of paper on the floor and have your youngster lie flat on it, on his back. Now trace his body with a magic marker. When you have finished draw in all the parts of the body. You even may wish to put clothes on your drawing. Pin up the masterpiece and, perhaps, make a second shadow drawing a few months later. The comparison between the two will help your child understand his development.

Just for fun lop off the head of the drawing. Take some pictures of your child standing behind the cut-out. Ask him what he would like to look like. Add clothes, muscles, etc. Keep snapping. Not only will you have fun, but you will also gain some insight into your child's perception of himself.

Privacy

"Teach your child that whatever his bathing suit covers is private." That may be a useful statement to be sure, however, most children do not understand the concept of privacy. Can you point to something in your child's environment that is totally his? Children do not own their toys; they have to share them with others. Nor do they own their clothes because from time to time they disappear and, a week later, may mysteriously turn up on little cousin Billy's back. They do not own their bedrooms which are constantly invaded by vacuum cleaners, guests and even baby sisters or brothers! Nor should we consider their favourite dolls or teddy bears as belonging to them, because they are perceived as individuals or separate beings that cannot be owned.

Give your child something that belongs only to him. A shoe box with his name written on it will do. Suggest that he put all his treasures into it. No one but he can touch the box without his permission.

Defend that little box against prying eyes. Respect it. Then show your child what possessions are private to you. "That jewellery box is mine. It is private. Please do not go into it without my permission." With vandalism on the rise, it is worthwhile to establish mutual respect for possessions at an early age.

Once the concept of privacy has been established as something tangible, the following rules will assume meaning:

"Whatever your bathing suit covers is private."

"No one has the right to make you feel uncomfortable."

If your children must share a room, find a way to establish private areas even within the more limited space of an apartment. You may, for example, put curtains around their bunk beds. If that is not possible, then perhaps a little time sharing may be required. This is helpful especially for older children who may have to share a room with a much younger brother or sister.

Contact With Strangers

While I am against using that old adage, "Don't talk to strangers," we, nonetheless, do not want our children talking to every Tom, Dick and Mary. And yet, beginning at birth, we will indirectly encourage them to do just that! This is the scenario:

Jennifer is fifteen months old. Decked out in Grandma's finest knits, she looks adorable when Mom takes her for a walk in the park. They meet Nice Lady who stops to admire beautiful Jennifer. Nice Lady says, "What a lovely child. What's her name?" Proud Mom says, "Thank you. Her name is Jennifer." "Hi Jennifer. Oh, she is cute. How old is she?" Mom replies, "She will be sixteen months on the fifth of this month."

Nice Lady might say, "Oh, she is a big girl. Hi, cutie. They are so sweet at this age." Mom knows better and says, "Oh, yes. But she is a handful. We are in an apartment over on Road Street. Apartments and kids don't mix well." "Yes, I know what you mean. I raised two of mine in apartments. What floor are you on?" Mom happily goes on. At some point, Nice Lady might say, "Does she talk?" Proud Mom says, "Oh yes. Say 'hi' to the nice lady Jennifer."

This is a typical conversation of a Mom out for a walk. In most respects, there is nothing wrong with being pleasant and, surely, our world has not deteriorated to such a state that we cannot say a cheery "hello" to another person. But what else has happened here? First, Mom has revealed a great deal of information about herself. Can you picture her going out for a walk without Jennifer, and saying to a complete stranger, "Hello, I have a sixteen-month-old daughter named Jennifer. I live on Road Street on the fourth floor . . ." Not likely.

The second thing that Mom did was encourage (or demand) that Jennifer perform for a stranger. Somehow, the child was given the idea that it is her role or duty to make Mom look good by responding to a stranger.

Most small children are gregarious and gracious beings. When out on a walk, they will greet mailboxes, say hello to dogs, and wave to strangers. This is normal behaviour for a secure and happy child. However, there is a vast difference between a child's display of natural exhilaration toward the world and a parent prompting the child to perform for the world.

"Don't take candy from strangers" is a hard rule to enforce should a child be offered a particularly tasty chocolate bar. Especially around holiday times, everyone seems to be handing out candy to children — the bankteller, the druggist, the receptionist at your office. Then, of course, there's Hallowe'en! It is difficult for us, as parents, to refuse offerings on behalf of our children, let alone tell them to say, "No."

If the child is under three, perhaps the best way to handle these situations is to intercept these gifts and give them out as treats from your own hand. Children over three should be encouraged to *check first* before they take anything from anyone. They must first ask someone who they trust. A simple turn of the head in the parent's direction may be all that is required.

Today, most of us feel strongly about children eating candy or other sweets. However, if your child has obeyed the rules and asked for permission, you may want to forego the anti-candy campaign for the moment in order to reinforce the more important streetproofing rule: Check first!

Safety First!

Streetproofing can be taught in captured moments that occur in everyday life. A small child often can decide she is lost in the shopping centre simply because Mom or Dad are not in her immediate field of vision. Mom may be two feet behind her but if the child thinks she is lost, she is! And when she lets out a loud wail, what is Mom's reaction? Does she rush up to the child and say, "For heaven's sake, I'm right here. Be quiet!" or "Hey, that is a loud noise. I bet you thought you were lost. I heard you and here I am."

Children who have been taught that the paramount objective in life is to be quiet, still, and polite, will not use their most effective weapon — their voice.

Model this for your child. If you are in a store and he wanders down an aisle, call out to him. Let him know that the roof will not collapse if he raises his voice.

Why do we teach our children to become so vocal? For one reason, of course, to attract attention, but also to scare off a would-be molester. Consider this. Why would anyone want to molest a loud, noisy child? Remember, we are teaching assertive, not aggressive behaviour. Like all things, this can be abused but better the behaviour suffers than the child. Yet, we do not want the child to scream blue murder because someone is coming her way. It is fair to say then, even to a young child, "If you are ever scared or feel that someone is trying to make you do something you do not want to do, scream. Do not worry about making a mistake or causing trouble. I will sort it out for you." We are, after all, our children's protectors and it is up to us to put things right. By the same token, we want them to respond to their instincts without fear of retribution.

While few people suggest using a harness on a small child as a matter of course, it is not out of place in a shopping mall, on a busy street, or in a parking lot. Should a parent initially be embarrassed about using the device, try putting it under an oversized T-shirt, cutting a hole in the back of the shirt to attach the reins.

Possibly, the most dangerous place for a child is a parking lot. Picture this, you have parked the car, got out, circled the car, taken baby out of the car seat, and placed her on the ground. What is the next physical action of the parent? Most of

40

us will turn back to the open car to retrieve a bag or purse or, at the very least, to lock the doors. A baby between one and three is capable of outdistancing an Olympic sprinter. Parents know that. That is why a harness is mandatory. Keep it on your child. When the reins are not in use, carry them in your bag or tuck them into the child's back pocket.

Safety Books

While teaching our youngsters the names of various types of birds, dinosaurs, and other creatures, why not add the names of current automobile models? We tend to spend an exorbitant amount of time teaching them what a "moo-cow" says, but ignore the fact that cars and roads play a far greater part in their lives.

Making up word books can be fun. Book I, suitable for infants up to 18 months, should be a simple, spiral-bound plastic scrapbook with pictures of a truck, a jeep, a convertible, a station wagon, a hardtop, a van, etc. Not only are the pages of these books easy to turn, but they are also washable, sturdy and, of course, the pictures can be interchanged.

Book II might contain actual pictures of model cars. Stop in at your local car dealer and begin a collection of glossy prints. It will not be long before your three-year-old knows more about cars than you do.

The streetproofing reason for teaching children about motor vehicles is simply that their street awareness will be enhanced and they may become more respecting of automobiles.

Imagine too, this scenario involving a seven-year-old: "Mommy, a funny thing happened today. A man in a blue Ford Capri, I think it was a '76, pulled up beside the park and you know what? He didn't have any pants on. How 'bout that?" While it is unlikely that the police will act upon a description coming from a young child, they will at least pay attention and be on guard.

The educational reasons for knowing the models of cars are boundless. Suggestions have even been made to teach children how to memorize license plate numbers. That, in itself, does no harm. However, if a child is in a threatening position involving a car, he had better rely on instincts and get away. Small children or those under ten should not be encouraged to spend precious moments looking at a mud-covered license plate or scratching numbers in the mud. They should leave the area quickly, preferably in the opposite direction of the car. A description of the car, its model and colour are enough evidence for a young child to provide at a later date.

Use another scrapbook to collect pictures of animals, dog breeds in particular. Dog bites are a frequent hazard. A child who has been bitten by an animal and can accurately describe it might save himself and his parents endless worry and pain.

Modern families often are dispersed. No longer do grand-parents live around the corner, and aunts and uncles down the block. Frequently, children see their relatives only on holidays. At those times, they are expected to greet them as old friends. Instead, they are known strangers, and the child might not want to be hugged or kissed by them. Respect that, give your child time. Having pictures of these people may help lessen initial hesitance.

You may want to provide your child with her own family scrapbook — a book that belongs to her. Page 1 might have a picture of her and the inscription, "This book belongs to Sally." Page 2 might have a picture of Mom when she was preg-nant with Sally. (Such a picture may lead to an early discussion of the facts of life). On Page 3, we may see Sally, Mom and Dad leaving the hospital. Perhaps, Pages 4 and 5 could show Mom and Dad when they were little. On Page 6 and so on, there may be pictures of the grandparents, the aunts and the uncles. On and on goes the book, each page relating to the child. Magic markers, construction paper and stickers all help to add colour and texture.

If you are a particularly creative parent, you may want to draw a family tree on the child's bedroom wall and hang on it pictures glued to wood or cardboard circles. Attach them with small picture hooks. When Grandma calls from Calgary, simply remove the picture and let the child hold it while she talks to her on the phone.

The streetproofing reason for such a measure is to allow a child to actually see where she fits into the scheme of things. It will increase her security and show her that she has resources. It is good to know that there are many people who love her and will help if things go wrong. If someone asks a child, "Who would you go to for help?'' the response usually is, ''My Mom.'' What if Mom is not around or if she is the abuser? Another reason why a child will benefit from graphically seeing her resources.

Include in the scrapbook or on the family tree pictures of your own close friends. As our family units change, our children begin to regard our friends as their extended family. These best friends often take on the responsibilities once performed by biological aunts and uncles and they even may be addressed that way.

These ideas are particularly important for children living in single-parent household. They too, need to see that they are part of a family structure.

The ''Who do you Love'' Game:

Ask your child this simple question, ''Who do you love?'' He will respond initially by saying, ''I love Mommy.'' ''I love Daddy.'' ''I love Bobby.'' He might rattle off a list of all the people he knows. Help him define ''like'' and ''love.'' It is a prelude to defining ''friends'' and ''acquaintances.''

Children see their world as a black and white place. When they are angry, do not be surprised to hear them say, ''I don't love you, I hate you.'' Here is how you can respond to the remark. ''You feel really mad at me because I won't let you have any candy. I can understand that. You probably don't like me one little bit. I still love you, though.''

Then, turn the question around and ask the child, ''Who loves you?'' If he is not very verbal but you happen to have a family tree on the wall or a scrapbook on the table, ask him to point to all the people who love him.

What Small Children Should Know:

1. Find a way to teach your children your first and last names. You may occasionally allow them to call you by your first name. If that bothers you, repeat your full name often. Ask him: ''What is my other name?'' ''What is Daddy's other name?''

2. It would not surprise parents to find out that their two-and-a-half-year-old knows the names of all the characters on Sesame Street. Yet, most of us assume that the same child can-

not learn her telephone number. Teach it by simple repetition while doing dishes or making beds. As soon as your child has mastered the seven magic digits, teach her your area code, address and, if applicable, her apartment number.

You may try setting your phone number to music and singing it. Simply assign one note to each digit and burst into song. If you can play an instrument, all the better.

3. While Punch and Judy are dated names, using puppets to tell a story or teach an idea are still valuable tools for parents to utilize.

Work out a mini-play with two puppets. One may want the toy the other one has. Punch says, "Gimme, gimme", and Judy says, "Mine, mine." Ask your child, "Who should have the toy? How do you think Punch feels? How do you think Judy feels?" As the show progresses, introduce new ideas, perhaps by using a third puppet who might ask Punch or Judy to do something that's not quite right. We also can have the third puppet (Mr. Smith) play tricks on the others (Judy).

Mr. Smith: "Wanna play a game?"

Judy: "Sure, I love games."

Mr. Smith: "OK. Take off all your clothes."

Puppeteer (from behind the stage): "Oh-oh. That's a funny game. What do you think of that? What should Judy say to Mr. Smith?"

Note: Rotate the puppets so that one of them is not all bad or all good all the time. If this is too confusing, have one "child" puppet remain the constant. Rotate the others.

There are many puppet-making books on the market. Hand-made puppets can be a lot more fun than bought ones.

VI

CREATIVE STREETPROOFING FROM THREE TO SIX

By the oh-so-tender age of three, most children will either have been in a day care centre for some time, or they will shortly be introduced to a nursery school situation. While parents remain the main protectors, increasingly, the child is left in the care of other persons.

Survival Kits

All children should have some sort of identification when they are outside the home. Very small children could carry a note in their pockets, even while out on a shopping trip with parents. Those who go to playschool or day care centre also could have a survival pack. They do not have to be able to read or dial a telephone in order to use it, however when lost, they must be told to give the pack to a salesperson, a Block Parent, a police officer and/or, in a pinch, to another mother.

The kit should be small, durable, perhaps even washable. It should contain an explanation and the child should be made aware of uses and misuses. Depending on the age of the child, we could say:

> "Christopher, Mommy has a purse and Daddy has a wallet. We carry an identification in our purses and wallets. Here is a little packet in which you can carry *your* identification. Mom and Dad take care of theirs, so you must too. If you lose it, come and tell me so I can replace it."

To start with, this usually is enough information. The next day or a week later you could add:

"If you are ever separated from me in a store, I think it would be best if you gave this little packet to a saleswoman."

Expand the explanation as the child gets older:

"Our phone numbers are in this packet along with quarters. Give me a call, or call your Dad at work . . ."

The survival kit should contain:

1. *An identification card*. Children and adults have a tendency to lose their identifications; as such you may want to omit the child's address. People who find the kit or the child seldom will deliver either to the owner or parent. Most people use the telephone.

2. *A list of telephone numbers*. Include your home phone number, the parents' work numbers, the number of a close friend who is likely to be at home most days; the number of the child's grandparents or godparents.

3. *Money*. It is not a good idea to put large amounts of money in this kit. Perhaps, when your child is older, you may want to give her taxi money to be used for emergencies but, for the time being, quarters for the telephone will suffice. If it becomes known that a child carries money, she may well be at risk from other children.

4. *Medical information*. Naturally, if your child has a medical problem or is allergic to certain drugs, he will have on him a medical alert tag. Regardless, include this information on paper and tuck it into the pack because children have a way of disposing of Medic Alert tags. Include the name of the child's pediatrician or general practitioner.

5. *Band-Aids*. Handing a child a survival kit could be intimidating. By including a Band-Aid, we are attempting to drive home the point that the kit can *prevent* problems.

6. *Love note*. If your child can read a little, stick in a note from you that says, "I love you." If she is lost, she will need some comfort. We also want her to be as much in control of the situation as possible. After all, we are talking about a very young child.

Jogger key cases are good choices for survival kits. They

are usually brightly coloured and compact in size. But they also can be quite expensive and if price is a problem, visit a sports store to see what they look like. Then make one yourself, better still a few extra ones!

The Pay Phone

Children should be taught how to use a pay phone. Although the task is above the heads of most three-year-olds, by the time they reach four and a half to five years, they are ready to practise. Head for the nearest pay phone and phone home. Phone Grandma too! Have fun. Keep up the practice. A dozen calls at different times are not too many. Teaching a four-year-old the mechanics of long-distance dialing may prove too difficult, so show her how to dial 0.

Most telephones in booths are too high for a child to reach. This is unfortunate and poses a problem. Point out the phones designed for handicapped people.

Good Touch, Bad Touch

Small children can tell what a good touch is. How can they tell? They know what is is like to be nursed, cuddled, held and hugged. What they need from us is our permission to refuse a bad touch.

Example:

"We got into an elevator on the 15th floor. By the time we reached the tenth, the elevator was packed and my two-and-a-half-year-old daughter and I were separated by a few feet. I looked around and saw her crushed against an older man who had his hands on her hair. He was talking to her. What looked to be his wife and adult granddaughter were with him. They were all telling my daughter how cute she was but the look on her face was not a happy one. I caught her eye and saw she was asking for help.

"For some stupid reason, I was more concerned about the effects my intervention would have on this older man than I was about my child. I didn't want him to think he was a molester or anything. He and his family seemed rather nice. And yes, maybe I was a little embarrassed too. I mean, no real harm was being done. Later, I told my daughter that she could have asked the man to stop touching her, but the words were lost on her."

Children must hear parents say "no" to some people. If Mom is a pushover for every salesperson who comes to the door the child may well be, too. If Dad cannot quietly and definitely stand up for his rights, the child will have difficulty standing up for hers.

Is your child allowed to say "no" without being called insolent and rude? Try out this little game with your three-, four-, or five-year-old:

The "No" Game:
Parent: "Every time I ask you a question, I want you to say no, OK? Here we go. Would you like a liver and pickle milkshake for lunch?"
Child: "No."
Parent: "Good. Now pretend I'm someone you don't know very well; here, I'll put on this hat. Would you like to come with me? I have some candy in my car."
Child: "No."
Parent: "Excellent. Here is another: My cat just had kittens. Would you like to see them?"
Child: "Little kitty cats?"
Parent: "Yes, little kitty cats."
Child: "OK."

The beauty of this game is that even small children can allow their imaginations to work. At some point, a second and harder lesson can be introduced. We must say that the word "No" does not have to be qualified. Children easily fall victim to adult reasoning powers if they do not understand just saying "No" is enough:

Adult: "Hey kid, want a ride?"
Child: "No, thank you."
Adult: "It's cold out there. Get in."
Child: "I'm not allowed to get into cars with strangers."
Adult: "Did your Mom say that? I bet she did. I bet she

doesn't like it when you get cold either. I bet she'd be happy if you were warm.''

So often, we are forced to say no to our child; ''No, don't touch that electric outlet;'' ''No, don't pull the dog's ears.'' By playing the ''No'' Game, we are putting the word ''No'' into positive context. Do I believe a very young child will put the game into practice? Probably not. We are giving assertive training here.

There are other ways we can encourage our child to stand up for his rights and say no. We all want children to share; it is part of socialization. If your child is having a hard time learning to share his toys, for example, ask her to pick out one toy and say, ''This is a toy you don't have to share because it is special to you. If someone else wants to play with it, you can say 'no, please don't play with my special toy.' '' Not only is this a good way to encourage a child's use of No, it also helps her to understand territory and privacy.

Is your child allowed to say No to you? Will you respect his right to do so? What if Aunt Martha comes for a visit? Is he allowed to shake hands with her or is must he kiss Aunt Martha?

Showing affection is natural for children, but you must allow them to decide to whom and how they want to display this affection. Don't force them to hug or kiss just anyone.

Example:

''My closest childhood friend moved back from British Columbia with her husband and three-year-old. I was thrilled. On the day the moving truck was to arrive, I offered to come over and care for Andrea. We had a marvellous time. I don't have children of my own and truly enjoyed being with her. That evening, more friends were invited for a house warming and Andrea was brought out in pyjamas to say good night. Her parents insisted she kiss everyone in the room, but the child really wanted no part of this bizarre ritual.

''When she came to me, I said, 'Why don't we shake hands?' The hoopla over that suggestion was astonishing. 'Give

Aunt Deb a kiss, go on, kiss her,' repeated Mother. I was so embarrassed. Finally, I put my foot down and said, 'No, Andrea does not have to kiss me.' I have not been invited back since.''

Shaking hands, a wave, a polite goodbye, all are alternatives to kissing that respect children's feelings and still conform to social norms.

When meeting children, we have a tendency to touch them, pat their hair, give them a hug. It would be a shame to cease the practice altogether. They need physical contact from those around them, however, if we touch, and they draw away, we must respect their right to do so without taking offense.

Do Not Advertise Their Names

In this age of awareness we only seldom find children who walk around with their names on their backs. Instead, we see names printed on barrettes, shoelaces, pencil boxes, jewellery, lunch pails, note pads, etc. Not long ago, I was at the zoo and met a little girl who was lost. I had no trouble finding out who she was. She was clutching a balloon with her name on it!

Why do we not want our children to walk around advertising their names? Picture this scenario:

Little Girl in the Park with name on necklace. "Hi, are you Jessica?" Little Girl looks up expectantly. "Yes." "You sure have grown since the last time I saw you. I remember when you could hardly talk. Did you get a Cabbage Patch Doll for Christmas?" "No, I got one for my birthday." "Oh, that's right. Your Mom told me about it. I'm on my way to see your Mom, wanna' come with me?" "I'm not supposed to go with strangers." "You are right. Good girl. But, I am going over to your house . . ."

Although this child knew her streetproofing rules she still was drawn into a conversation. Why? By seeing her name on the necklace, our stranger found a crack in Jessica's armour.

Know Your Area

I would like to again discuss the importance of taking walks with children around your own neighbourhood. Small children can lose themselves quite easily. A common scene takes place in a bank, for example, when a child wanders off a few feet and reaches for the hem of what seems a familiar skirt. What a surprise it is to look up and see that it belongs to a stranger.

Children can and need to understand their territory. We may begin this learning process by allowing them to lead the way home. This seems simple enough, but those under five still can lose themselves by straying only a few feet off the beaten track. To help them become familiar with their own area, consider doing the following:

a. Vary the route you take to a much-frequented destination.

b. Point out landmarks, making a game of which one comes next.

c. Spot your house or apartment building from different angles, for instance, from a neighbour's window.

d. Tell your child to close her eyes and imagine her surroundings.

e. Listen to sounds. We live in a noisy age, yet we seldom hear the sounds around us. Play the listening game. Repeat all the sounds you hear. Is there a church nearby? Can you hear the bells? Are there airplanes overhead? Trains coming down the tracks? Are you near a highway? A hospital? A school?

Circle of Privacy

The space that surrounds our bodies is our own. It belongs to us. As adults we all know when our space is being invaded. A person comes up too close to speak to us and we step back. Should someone by moving into our space become sexually aggressive we hear the message loud and clear.

We can encourage children to value and protect *their* personal space. Have your child stand up and together reach forward, upward, downward, and behind you. Now turn around and examine the space from this angle, physically feeling it.

Make the exercise a game and say, "This is my space, show me yours." Once the physical form of the circle of privacy has been understood, explain to the child that no one has the right to come into it, unless he says so.

Expect a lot of questions, such as, "Mommy, Tommy stepped into my personal space. Tell him not to." A possible retort might be, "It is up to you to tell people to stay out of your space. However, if someone bigger than you steps into it and makes you feel uncomfortable, then tell me." Another question might be, "Tommy won't give me a hug cause he says he can't come into my space." Things can get confusing . . .

Ask your child to name times when we have to share our personal space. Remind him of certain social occasions — standing riding a crowded subway or bus, in a line-up, etc.

As your child grows up and gets accustomed to the idea of preserving a circle of privacy, you may want to talk about keeping at arm's length and staying even a bit further away from anyone he does not know well. This becomes a little complicated at times, because while we want our children to keep a distance from people, we don't want them to walk about with outstretched arms that can be pulled or grabbed.

Here is another game you can play: Have your child stand still in the middle of the room. Go to the door and then slowly walk toward him. Let him tell you when to stop. The idea is to say "stop" exactly one meter away. Take a ruler and measure. A playschool or day care centre also can play this game and children on their own will have fun with it as well. They will learn to understand personal space and develop a concept of distance.

Self-defense, I

Inevitably, when we think of self-defense for young children, we envision a group of miniature karate experts zipping around a gym, throwing each other over their right hips, breaking six-inch boards and yelling, 'Hi-Ya." In reality, self-defense means such simple things as "walk on the green and not in between," answering or not answering the door, responding to questions over the telephone, putting away roller skates, and maintaining composure in stressful situations. Self-defense is always with us, just as taking care and taking precautions is. We can help children understand that and the meaning of self-defense by drawing attention to our actions. For example, when driving a car, we can point out road hazards, explain why we don't pass on the inside lane, why we signal to other cars, and much more! Everyday events will allow us to explain a variety of self-defense practices.

When we think of self-defense, we also think of physical assertiveness. Small children learn to assert themselves positively through past and present accomplishments. In fact, any task a child does well adds to her self-esteem as well as to her physical prowess. Listed below are ways to encourage children to continue on this healthy track:

a. Mothers need to roughhouse with their children. It is not uncommon to see Dad on a Saturday afternoon playing tag or catch with them. Nor is it unusual to see him brawl with his kids on the front lawn or in the park while the dog leaps on top of him. But where is Mom? She is in the house doing whatever it is Moms do in the house. Moms need to get dirty, too. They can catch a ball, tackle Dad, crawl under a fence, and laugh while doing it. Moms can best show their daughters that it is alright to be physically active, to take the initiative, to win and to lose. A son also needs to see his Mom as physically assertive.

b. While romping around with our children, we can oh-so-gently introduce the idea of physical defense. Before we continue, let me dispell a few myths. We do not need a black belt in karate to teach small children some basic self-defense moves. Nor do we have to overexplain the reasons why we are showing them these things. If all this is done within playtime and with a smile, children will assume it is just more fun stuff. Certainly, at a later stage, it would be useful to take a self-defense course, but initially all we need is a dose of common sense and an ability to read our children's characters.

c. Within the context of playtime and without referring to self-defense, we can teach the child how to break the hold another person might have on her. Grab her arm or shoulder and help her twist out of your grasp. You want her to spin around and around as quickly as possible. While she does it, encourage her to yell out. Once she has broken your grasp or more likely you have let go, tell her to run. "Hurray! Look at you go! No one could hold you for long!" With more practice, she will be able extricate herself easily, providing you don't hold her in a half nelson! If both parents are participating, the child can get away from the one and run into the open arms of the other and vice versa.

I do not believe for one moment that a child can foil a deliberate, hostile attack. A five-year-old is simply too small to stop a 180-pound adult. On the other hand, if she behaves aggressively when grabbed she has on her side the element of surprise.

d. What are some other things a five-year-old can do to prevent abduction? He can go limp, (show him how), roll on the ground, kick and scream, and make a general nuisance of himself. Best of all, he can be told that it's OK to run away from a situation which makes him feel uncomfortable.

e. Encourage your youngsters to participate in those sports once designated as being in the "male only" domain. Many parents do not approve of young children engaging in aggressive team sports and I am among them. However, this should not preclude a game of pick-up soccer or baseball. Perhaps, there are sports organizations in your area which are run for fun and exercise. If you choose to enroll your child in such activities, stay with him. Do not leave the area or the field.

Body Language

While not an exacting science, body language may sharpen a child's awareness, his instincts and, by learning to explain different emotions, develop his verbal skills. The following exercises can be done in the home, in a day care centre, a nursery school, etc. They are particularly helpful when dealing with hearing-impaired or similarly handicapped children.

Exercise No. 1:
Cut out magazine pictures showing:
- a child crying
- a family laughing
- people hugging
- people fighting, etc.

Mount the pictures on cardboard. Now hold up each one and ask your child:
"What is this person feeling?"
"Why do you think this person is happy, sad . . .?"

Exercise No. 2:
   Now find some photographs showing:
   • a homecoming
   • a wedding
   • a funeral
   • children fighting
   • children playing
   • an accident.
   Again, mount each picture on cardboard and ask your child:
   "What is happening in this picture?"
   "What happened just before the picture was taken?"
   "What do you think will happen next?"
   "Can you make up a story about this picture?"

   With these exercises we want to examine body language and behaviour, as well as encouraging storytelling.

Exercise No. 3:
   Look for pictures that portray a baby crying and a mother talking on the telephone, or people sitting around a campfire smoking cigarettes. To start off, you might try drawing a few fun examples such as a fish with feet, a horse with a bunny's tail, a house with arms, a car with wings. Now ask the child, "What is wrong with this picture?" Once children understand what it is they are looking for, it will be easy to follow up with a more complicated version of the exercise.

Exercise No. 4:
   Clip out magazine pictures of different people, such as a man, a woman, a family, a group of women or children. Now ask your child, "Which person(s) would you go to if you and I were separated from each other while out shopping?" Often a child will point to a picture because the particular person in it "looks like Uncle Rob, so he must be nice." Talk to your child about her choices and bring back her attention to the pictures showing mothers with small children.*

Exercise No. 5:
   All children enjoy "Felt-board Storytelling." If you do not

*My thanks to Kathy Hawkins for this suggestion.

have a flannelboard in your home, buy a meter or two of dark felt and staple it to a lightweight board. Presto! You have a felt storytelling board.

If you are handy with scissors, cut human shapes out of coloured felt, or simply dig up more magazine pictures and back them with bits of felt. Now walk your felt people across the board, through all sorts of situations. Take them to the zoo, across a street, around the neighbourhood.

Exercise No. 6:

Make a storytelling apron using a kitchen apron. Stash all the felt characters (or pictures) into the pockets. Then place on the board a child character and ask your child to reach into your pocket and pull out another felt person and place him/her on the board next to the child character. Should the child talk to this new person? What if that person moved closer to the child? What should the child do? Is the new person nice, good, bad, etc . . .

Exercise No. 7:

Pick up some road safety pamphlets. Many of them will contain pictures of traffic signs, i.e. stop signs, children-crossing signs, etc. Mount the pictures on your felt board and have the child obey the signs.

It will not be long before you have built up quite a collection of felt friends with whom your child will enjoy playing.

The Staring Game

We cannot read kids' minds, yet we often tell them we know what they are thinking. When we say, "Mom has eyes in the back of her head," we also lead them to believe that we know what they are doing. It is, therefore, not surprising that children who experience sexual molestation at a young age assume we know about it.

When you play the staring game with your children, chances are you will only have to play it a few times as once learned, they will teach it to others.

Sit opposite your child and stare at her. Have her stare back at you. The first one to break eye contact loses. Now ask her why the eye contact was broken. Because the eyes got tired, laughter interfered and, oddly enough, even small children can blush. Now, try to guess what the other is thinking. You can't. "No one can tell what you are thinking or feeling unless you tell someone. Sometimes we think we can guess what a person is thinking, but we can't really be sure. Want to try the game again?" Having understood that the eyes are not windows to the mind, the child will, no doubt, become quite proficient at the game. A valuable streetproofing lesson will have been learned along the way.

VII

CREATIVE STREETPROOFING FROM SIX TO TEN

Somewhere, somehow, our baby has disappeared forever. Across the breakfast table sits an imposter, perhaps a fantastic little individual but an imposter, nevertheless. Children between the ages of six and ten appear to be rather competent little people. They are, however, and will remain for a while — children. Between six and ten they are, for the first time, out and about on their own. Vulnerable to peer pressure, bullies, coersion, bribery, and all those other "normal" things found in every schoolyard, they are at an age when a parent either can or cannot instill the values that will last a lifetime.

Make A Map

We have discussed going for walks with small children, but now it is time to put your area on a map that shows every likely or unlikely path or street your child might take. Note where the alleys are, Block Parents homes, etc. Include potentially dangerous areas, such as construction sites, hydro relay stations and towers.

For the map consider using the back of an old shower curtain. Mark it up with coloured pens and stickers. Pin it up in the family room or other convenient place expanding it as the child's territory expands.

You might ask the neighbourhood kids to help out or you could suggest it to your pre-school as a class project.

If planning such an exercise is too time-consuming for you, try making the map in a sandbox with your child. Mark off home in the sand, then the park. Discuss how you get there.

Or, you may want to make a colour-coded map. Take one green, one black, one red and one orange crayon or marker, and draw on a large piece of paper your street in black. Add the houses, the park and, let's say, a shopping centre at the end of your street. Colour all "safe" houses green, i.e. your own, that of a neighbour you know well, and the Block Parents' home(s). Colour the park orange. Why? It is an area where to use caution. If you do not want your child to go to the shopping centre, colour it red for danger.

Self Defense, II

We already have discussed some aspects of physical self-defense, however, when applied between the ages of six and ten, we can truly take a great leap forward.

Before we race out to enroll Junior in a self-defense course, let us look why we want to teach him. We are not trying to create pint-sized Marines nor are we attempting to make our children into small street warriors, but we would like to build up self-confidence in their minds and bodies.

Before signing up for lessons check out the school's credentials. Drop in on classes. (This not only applies to self-defense, but to all activities in which we enroll our children — Girl Guides, Boy Scouts, ballet lessons, piano lessons, etc.).

As with all aspects of streetproofing, you do not want to go overboard. Balance. Perhaps, you prefer not to deal with physical or class-oriented self-defense at all. You might find the idea of an eight-year-old boy or girl learning the martial arts distasteful, too violent. To force him or her into such a situation without your full approval would, in all likelihood, be counterproductive. If, however, you are considering the idea, remember we are educating our children for a world we do not know, preparing them for experiences we cannot imagine. We teach them how to read to further develop their minds, so that they can play an active role in our society. We teach them self-defense skills so that they can protect their bodies and be self-confident. On the home front, we may encourage the idea by simply telling them that they have the right to defend themselves.

We can begin by playing tag. When the game gets boring or just before you collapse from exhaustion, add a new element. Call this activity "catch." Have the child run, catch her, and pin her down. Now say, "If you wanted to get away, it would be OK to fight, really fight." Show her your weak spots — the eyes, the groin, etc. Explain that under no circumstances is she allowed to engage in this activity with other children. Children must be told that when they are in danger they can use whatever is available to them — a stick, sand, etc.

Sitting on the grass, we can gently introduce self-defense, pointing out that while this activity may have started out as a game, it is, in reality, not a game we play with other children for fun. While the two of you may be having fun at that moment, you actually are teaching her a way to be safe.

Parents must tread lightly here. If you have an assertive child, you probably will have no trouble introducing "catch" around the six-year-old mark. For parents of less assertive children it may be better to hold off for a while.

The most effective defense a child can have is to run away. While we want to encourage physical assertiveness, we do not want him to feel that he can win in a physical contest with an adult. If your son states categorically that he can indeed beat up any bad guys, it will be necessary to show him that he simply cannot. Emphasize that people who run away are not cowards, but simply people who use common sense to protect themselves.

Example:

"My husband and I took our two boys to a movie on a summer evening. We were late for the show and couldn't find a parking spot. In the end, we parked in an alley behind a restaurant. Our youngest son became ill during the show, so we decided to leave early. As we turned into the alley, we saw several big boys remove the sound system from our car. My husband and I instinctively took the boys' hands and kept walking down the main street until we reached a phone booth. They must have sensed our actions because neither of them called out or said a word. We phoned the police and went to a nearby restaurant to wait.

"A while later, my husband left and I remained in the restaurant with the boys. They didn't say much at first, but finally our eight-year-old asked me why Daddy had not stopped those men from stealing. I explained that it would have been dangerous for him to do so.

"Everywhere we turn, our children are being told that bravery is beating up someone. It occured to me that there was not one television show that my boys *liked* that did not pit good against evil.

"The conversation did not end there. We talked a great deal about bravery and cowardice. We did our best to explain that truly brave people are those who defend other people from hurt, not possessions.

"It was unfortunate that our car was broken into, however I would say we were very fortunate. This one incident led to other useful discussions with our children on such topics as racism, bigotry, and the rights of the individual.

Safety in the Parking Lot

Here is an idea that you might want to try out with an older, very secure child. Let us say, the two of you are in the parking lot of your local shopping centre. You are coming out the doors of the store carrying $100.00 worth of groceries in four bags. Walking toward your car, say something like, "If I were grabbed right here, I wonder what I would do?" Don't expect an immediate response. Most children would say, "You should run." That would be a good answer, to be sure, and while you would compliment your child, you still might say, "What else could I do?"

Other responses might be, "Go back to the store." You could persist by saying, "Whoever is attacking me is in my way; anyway, the store is a long way from here." Look around. Think along with your child. Now, look down under the cars. Whenever possible, we want answers to spring directly from the children to develop their thinking process, in the hope that in future they will come up with their own correct answers, instead of trying to remember what Mommy said.

"You'd get under a car and scream."

"Right. I'd drop all my packages because who cares about food or anything else at a time like this. Yes, I'd get under a parked car and keep screaming. You really are getting good at this streetproofing stuff, aren't you?"

A very simple lesson would have been completed here without fear. Imagine trying to teach the same lesson in the living room! Not being able to project or imagine the layout of a parking lot, it is unlikely for a child to come up with the desired answer.

The Password

Passwords are used to help children identify people who have been sent by Mom or Dad to pick them up. Here is an example of when a password may be used:

Neighbour: "Amanda, your Mom has a flat tire. She can't come to get you. Get in the car and I'll drive you home."
Child: "What's the password?"
Neighbour: "Chicken Noodle Soup."
Child: "OK."

This may sound like a great streetproofing idea, and passwords have been known to work beautifully. All too often, however, families initiate them but after a few weeks forget about them because they cannot cope with the many exceptions to the rule. They may find themselves saying to the child, "You can go with so-and-so and of course with so-and-so." Pretty soon, the only people left out are strangers, and the child is not supposed to go with them, anyway.

Those of us living in a big city probably would find the use of a password more effective than people living in a small town. This is not to suggest that country children are any less at risk than city children. However, in most smaller communities relatives are closer at hand, and parents tend to delegate child care responsibility to neighbours and other family members, more often than city folk do.

If you choose to use a password, do so with commitment and diligence. Children must be told that this is a special word and to please keep it to themselves.

Pick a word that is simple, memorable and has meaning in your children's lives. Better still, let them pick it. If you have more than three children, you may want to have one word for all of them, changing it periodically.

There are times when a password is a must. If you feel that your child is at risk, particularly because of a possible non-custodial abduction, use the word without fail.

Make a Bill of Rights

We may repeatedly tell our children that they have the right to their own bodies, the right to be heard, to protect themselves, to say "no." However, these are the words a child hears. We need to give them more than our verbal approval of self-protection. We need to take these words and put them into graphic form.

Here is the Constitution I drew up for our home. Not all the documented rights will be acceptable to you, nor will they necessarily apply to your life. You may feel I have gone too far, or not far enough, but having read my example, you may wish to sit down with your family and write your own Bill of Rights.

THE CONSTITUTION OF THE McKAY/MacLEOD HOUSEHOLD

These are the rights of every member of this house. We will stand by them, respect them, and demand all those who cross this threshold or come into contact with us respect them too.

1. We have the right to protect ourselves in any manner we think necessary.

2. We have the right to say NO.

3. We have the right to be heard and ask questions on any topic.

4. We have the right to privacy and private time.

5. We have the right to ask for help and get help.

6. We have the right to lie if our instincts tell us to.

7. We have the right to tell a secret.

8. We have the right to love and be loved.

SIGNED, _____ YEAR, _____

Notice the reference to *we* as opposed to *I*. This constitution is intended for the whole family. Responsibility to it and for it is, therefore, shared by all its members. While we may add to it in the future, it is designed to last us a lifetime.

Writing a similar list of rights will enable you to discuss with your children topics you may otherwise not have touched when talking about protection. Explain each right and take care to record all of them in easy-to-read and understandable language. Ask for input.

You may even wish to have these rights printed on parchment and framed. This is a great idea and will give your constitution the status it deserves. However, it is meant to be a working tool, not an adornment for the family room wall. Keep it at hand and hang it at the eye level of your child. No doubt, after the initial excitement of making, signing, dating, framing and hanging it, it will be remembered as just another one of "Mommy's Projects." However, if it is ever needed, it will be there.

Answering the Telephone

Telephones are familiar instruments to young children. By the age of two, most of them will be babbling freely to Grandma and Grandpa. Those who have reached five or six years are ready to learn how to properly answer the phone.

We do want our children to be considerate of others, however, we certainly don't want them to be so friendly that they give out information over the telephone without first finding out who is calling.

Things can get tricky. If a caller asks to speak to Mom and, for some reason, she is not home, nor is Dad or the babysitter, we want our children to say, "Mom is busy at the moment. Can she call you back?" The comment that inevitably will pop up is, "But that is a lie!" At this stage, most parents panic. They find themselves winding down the garden path, dragging a six-foot explanation behind. Instead, we can state, "Perhaps it is a lie. Nevertheless, it is nobody's business where I am. So please, if someone calls, just say I'm busy."

A friend of mine started a small business at her neighbour's home, and she spends a good deal of time popping in and out of both houses. I called up one day and was told by her eight-year-old daughter "Mommy's out." Later that day, I had a chance to talk to my friend to tell her what her daughter had said.

A week later I phoned back and the little girl answered. "May I speak to your Mom?" I politely inquired. "Ah, Mom's in the bathroom. She's, ah . . . real constipated. She'll, ah . . . will be awhile."

Small children can dial a telephone. The better-quality push-button phones are decidedly the easiest for a child to operate, and the newer giant push-button types are an excellent idea if the budget allows. Avoid "cute" phones that are difficult to handle.

Naturally, the emergency phone numbers are posted by the telephone. You may want to clip out small pictures and place them next to these numbers. For example, beside the fire station number could be a picture of a fire truck; a policeman would match up with the police's number, and so on. Beside Dad's and Mom's office numbers, paste up their photographs. All these phone numbers now will be easier to decipher for children who know how to dial a phone and read numerals.

Washroom Mania

I've come to the conclusion that a high percentage of mothers have a phobia about men's washrooms, specifically about sending little boys into one of "those" places. The facility, contrary to public belief, is not a den of iniquity. All men, as a matter of fact, use public toilets for a specific and valid reason. Is this to suggest that we should allow Toddler John to make use of them?

At some point, usually between the ages of six and ten, our sons will attempt to exercise their rights. Going to the men's washroom alone is considered a rite of passage for little boys. We cannot ignore it.

Examples:
"The time had come. For months, my seven-year-old son had been pestering me about going to the washroom alone. We compromised. First, I allowed him to go into a cubicle in the women's washroom alone, then into the women's washroom by himself while I stood outside. One day, an elderly lady said to him, Aren't you big enough to go into the men's washroom? After that, he would not go back to the women's.

"One Saturday afternoon my son asked to go into the men's. Fine. I gave him instructions. He had three minutes. I posted myself at the entrance and waited. Three minutes passed, then five. I pushed open the door a crack and called out to him. No response. A young man came out. I asked him if he had seen a little boy in there. He shrugged and passed by. I was now nervous. I called again. No response. Then I thought, what if there is another exit? I flew in, calling out as I went.

"There must have been at least ten cubicles, all lined-up in a row with three urinals at the back. Three men stood in front of them. I started pounding on every cubicle door. One man came out, looking as if he would have a seizure on the spot. I came to the second to last cubicle. My neighbour came out. I was frantic. I pounded on the door of the last cubicle. The door popped open. There he was, sitting like a king! 'Why didn't you answer me?' I screamed. 'I wasn't finished,' he replied."

There you are in a movie house with three kids. They have their popcorn and drinks. The movie begins and one of them has to go to the washroom.

Do not allow children to go to a movie house washroom alone. Often, the mezzanine is deserted and even the popcorn people have left. Go with the child. Two children alone are safe. It is not always necessary to drag along the whole party. However, if you are not comfortable with leaving the children alone, by all means, take everyone with you.

Dad pulls up at the gasoline station. Child needs to go to the washroom. "Go get the key," says Dad and child scampers off. In my opinion, the only reason why the majority of gas station washrooms are locked is to keep the germs in. Besides, many of these conveniences are located at the back of the building backing on to an open field. If you must use such a washroom, go with the child.

- Do not allow your child to go into a washroom that has two exits.
- Teach your child how the locks work on cubicles. Some children may panic if they cannot open the door, but most will instinctively crawl under it.
- Little girls out with Dad are in a low-risk situation. Statistics show that women are not likely to molest. Dads have a tendency to ask other Moms for help. This is usually unnecessary. If your daughter is too old to go into the men's washroom, have her follow the rules we applied to boys — give her a time limit; tell her to call out if she is in trouble.
- If you don't want your child to talk to anyone, tell him to skip the handwashing. This is when a conversation is most likely to get started. Also, taps may be hard to

reach, and children who have trouble regulating the water temperature, may inadvertently scald themselves.

- Campground, subway, or street washrooms are places small children should not use alone. Encourage them to "buddy-up" when they are on their own.

Home Communications Centre

Perhaps, you can remember this statement from your own past: "Oh, Mother, I'm just going out, I don't know where we will end up." If you didn't say it yourself, there is a definite likelihood that one or all of your children will say it to you. Stressing responsibility to each other by all family members may help you deal with such statements at a later date.

In their book, *A Parent's Guide to Streetproofing Children*, Richard Gossage and Melvin Gunton describe the home communications centre as "a central place in your home where members of your family leave information pertaining to their day activities. This information should tell you or your children where any member of the family is at any given time. . . . The information centre allows the family to communicate with each other, when time and conflicting commitments don't allow for face-to-face meetings. It gives the family flexibility and, at the same time, demonstrates a concern for each other's well-being." (p. 154).

Locate such a centre near your telephone. The equipment needed is: a bulletin board and/or chalkboard, a day planner, a pen or pencil, and a short list of emergency phone numbers, prominently displayed and separate from other numbers. There is something else of equal importance: near the telephone post your own address, written in large letters. All too often, a babysitter, grandparent, or other caretaker have had to report an accident or fire, only to find that they were unable to remember the address of the house they were in.

On your day planner record the activities of all household members. Small children will benefit from watching the centre in action; they will derive a great deal of pleasure from seeing their names on the board and their activities recorded.

Near at hand, keep a copy of your child's fingerprints, as well as a list of physical characteristics — birth marks, scars, weight, height, colouring, etc. Find a picture of your child that really looks like him. The one we are after should be a black-and-white print that shows him standing or sitting alone. Such photos are easily transmitted over wire services. Tape the picture to the fridge or keep it in a prominent spot where you will be reminded to update it periodiclly.

Why should you go to all the trouble? Simply, to know where your child is should you ever have to call her home in an emergency. More importantly, should a child go missing we must know about it as soon as possible. How long do we have to wait before we can report a missing child to the police? Perhaps 24 hours? How about 48 hours? We do not have to wait at all! If something has gone wrong, if you *feel* something has happened, after having checked the usual places, call immediately. Trust your instincts!

What if you have called the police and your child turns up in the meantime, or worse, in the tracks of the police officers? To be a parent is to be in a constant state of embarrassment. From the moment we lie on the birthing table to the time we are shunted to the old folks home, our children will find more ways to embarrass us than we could ever have imagined.

Needless to say, no one should ever waste the police's time. However, if there is one instance when a police officer wants the case solved before it is opened, this is it. Finding a missing person is very difficult. That is why the police always responds. Should your young wanderer come home to find a constable outside his front door, the message of responsibility certainly will have been driven home.

Fingerprinting Children

Why do we fingerprint children? Many parents feel that this is a measure that somehow prevents abductions. It does not. Primarily, fingerprints are used to identify deceased persons. This may sound gruesome, but imagine *not* knowing if your child has died. Imagine trying to carry on a normal life, all the while thinking that she is somewhere out there and needs us. Can there be a greater depiction of living hell?

One lesser reason why we may want to have a child fingerprinted, is to facilitate identification of an older child who was abducted at any early age. In rare instances it may be possible for the police to dust for print in places where they suspect the child has been held. Such information would aid in tracking her down, as well as helping to build a case against the offender.

Most small children enjoy being fingerprinted. Occasionally, an older child will balk at the idea and if yours displays anxiety when confronted with the prospect, do not force the issue. Perhaps, she believes fingerprinting is only for criminals. If that is the case, have your own prints done. Let her watch.

Many organizations and/or private companies fingerprint children, however, beware of charlatans. There are no nationwide set standards for fingerprinting.

Basically, infants should be footprinted, children under three palmprinted, and those over three fingerprinted, — one finger at a time — using the roll method. Dipping a child's fingers into ink and transferring the imprints onto paper is a useless exercise.

School Trips

Sooner or later, the day will come when our children, although still young are virtually on their own. A class trip is just such an event. The initial feeling of most parents confronted with the prospect of letting their child go off with who-knows-who is, "my daughter will be sick on that day." On the other hand, these outings are wonderful and exciting. However, if you have valid doubts about the supervision of such an excursion, by all means, withdraw. Weigh the pros and cons carefully. Ask some questions:

1. Is it possible for you to come along as a helper? Few schools would refuse an offer of this type.

2. How many teachers and support staff will be accompanying the children?

3. How many roll calls or head counts will be taken? This is important. Don't let yourself be put off by the response, "As many as we think are required." Roll calls should be taken after the children leave each and every area they are visiting. For example, if they are at the zoo, a head count should be taken after leaving each pavilion. If they are on a walking tour, roll calls and head counts should occur *at least* every half hour.

4. What will the teacher do should a child be lost?

5. Do the teachers and staff know the layout of the area, or is this their first venture?

6. What rules concerning bathroom visits will be given to each child?

7. If there only are female teachers on the trip, what happens when a male child wants to go to the bathroom?

8. What time will the children arrive at their destination and what time will they leave for home?

9. What kind of ID will each child carry? All too frequently children are given great big name tags, usually in the shape of an apple or an elephant. Now wait a minute. We have all accepted the idea that we no longer will advertise our children's names on T-shirts and jackets! Why must we go along with the practice of having names across their chests? Suppose a child is lost, would he not become an easier target for a potential offender?

I asked one seasoned teacher why, given all the statistics on missing children, schools still persist in labelling children this way. Her response, "If a child is making too much noise, it's important to be able to call him or her by name." Crowd Control? We are talking about six- to ten-year-olds!

Identification is important, there is no denying that. Let us find a compromise. At the very least, the child can wear the name and number of her teacher. Her personal ID can be kept in her pocket.

Some day care centres or nursery schools may ask you to sign a blanket approval form allowing them to take the children for walks, to the fire hall, etc. I disapprove of such requests and policies. If an outing is planned approval can be obtained for each one. You may object to some and, certainly, as parents we have the right to know exactly where our children are and with whom.

Talk to your child about the forthcoming event, well in advance. Adequate preparations cannot be made overnight. In addition, take the following precautions:

1. Teach your child how to use a pay phone.

2. Equip her with a Survival Pack.

3. Survival Packs have a way of getting lost. Put extra identification in her pocket. If she is wearing a dress, pin a card to her underwear. (Use a diaper pin.)

4. Talk plainly and openly about the possibility of becom-

ing separated from the group. Talk about it without fear or threats.

5. Be available. Tell your child where you will be — at home, at the office, etc.

VIII

SEXISM

Why are female children more likely to be molested than male children? Sexual abusers do not necessarily choose their victims on the basis of the biological difference, yet girls are more at risk than boys because they are perceived to be more passive and less likely to put up a fuss. Combating sexism, therefore is an important part of streetproofing.

Small children are perhaps the biggest little sexists you are likely to meet. They like to put things and people into orderly little compartments.

One winter evening when two-year-old son Charlie was playing with his plastic boats in the bathtub, I asked him, "Do you think a woman could be captain of a ship?" Plainly and bluntly he replied, "No." Naturally, I was shocked, but persisted. "Do you think a woman could be a doctor?" Again he replied in the negative. "But, but . . . your Aunt Sonia is a doctor! Remember her white coat and stethoscope?" His reply, "Aunt Sonia, nurse." Hmmm. "Can a man take care of little children?" I asked. "Only Daddy" was his response. "Can a man wash dishes?" "No." I was becoming upset and flustered. "But Charlie, Mommy *never* does the dishes; Daddy does them." Perhaps he had not understood the question. Please. let that be the reason! "Can Daddy cook?" Charlie answered, "Mommy cooks," One more try: "Who drives a car?" He had to get this one. He must know I'm the better driver. Can you guess what Charlie's response was?

Where did my small son pick up all that nonsense? Feeling perturbed, I posed the same questions to a parenting group and asked them to put them to their own youngsters. They returned a week later as stunned as I had been.

Try this experiment: Ask your very young children these point-blank questions: "Can a woman be a truck driver?" "Can a man be a nurse?" "Can a woman play soccer?" "Can a woman be a firefighter?" (Note: A typical response to this last question is, "You mean, can a woman be a fireman?").

The well-known American author Alfred Toffler believes that we are raising children for a world we do not know and, in our wildest dreams, could never fathom. Many of us still have grandparents living. My own grandmother was born in 1897. She is a bright, beautiful woman who has seen more changes in her lifetime than anyone in a previous existence. She grew up wearing long skirts and travelling by horse and buggy, and now waits to tell my son — her great-grandchild — about such things as icemen, her uncle who fought in the Crimea, and about the first automobile she saw. She also has a story about the day she bought a radio and three men and a boy had to carry it up the stairs. She remembers when flying was in its infancy while sitting in her armchair to watch the space shuttle take off and land.

We no longer have the luxury of basing our parenting practices on the sexist rules of generations past. Our roles are changing at break-neck speed. Yet, while we prepare our children for the future, we also have to carry with us the sexist baggage with which we grew up: "Mommies make brownies and beds, Daddies don't."

Children did not create the world in which they live, they inherited it. Yet, the world of the future will bear little resemblance to the one we inhabit at present.

By necessity, there will be role changes. Future Moms no longer will keep up the pace of working outside and inside the home, as well as raising children. They won't tolerate such overwork. If we continue to raise our sons to be brave little soldiers, who are they going to fight? If we encourage our daughters to be dependent, sweet little things, what kind of life role can they expect to assume?

The poorest people in today's society are older women. Many find themselves destitute at age 65, 70, 90. Their crime? Most of them reared children and kept house. Could parents born in the 1850s have foreseen such a turn of events? Is it their fault that the babies they bore ended up in this situation? No. They taught little girls to sew, cook, and mind the children.

Can we project eight decades ahead? We cannot. But we can prepare our children for change by creating in both sexes agility, independence, flexibility, and love of life. By doing so, we will have better equipped them for the adult roles they will have to play one day.

In the future, parenting will be the concern of both Mom and Dad. You may feel you live in a household where Dad equally shares responsibilities with Mom. Try this test. If all responses to the following questions are "yes" you indeed are in a uniquely equal parenting situation:

1. Who picks the babysitter? Day care centre?
2. Who buys the children's clothes?
3. Who brushes the children's hair?
4. Who makes doctors' appointments?
5. Who balances the diet with high fibre content?
6. Who decides when it is time to start toilet training?
7. Who reads streetproofing books?
8. Who gave birth? (Just couldn't help myself!)

Equal parenting is never equal.

When we talk about sexism, inevitably, the accent is placed on raising female children to view themselves as *equals*. Our male children deserve the same attention.

Housework has long been a point of contention in many homes. A common statement from a "liberated" Dad is, "Oh, I help out a lot. I do the dishes, I do the vacuuming . . ." Think about the words, "help out." They imply choice, a favour that is being done. In effect, what is being said is, "Housework is something we do when we feel like it but when we don't, Mom will do it."

During the past year, while lecturing on streetproofing, I often touched upon the topic of sexism. While it deserves a full-length lecture, at the very least, I had to restrict myself to one simple suggestion: Little boys *need* dolls! Not one of those busty, blond abominations, but baby dolls they can nurture and care for. And when we see our three-year-old tuck in his baby he needs to hear us say, "You are going to make a good Daddy one day." This seemingly obvious idea often is met with the response, "Oh, I'd allow my son to have a doll but my husband would never permit it."

We go to great lengths to teach Eldest Daughter how to feed and change the new baby. Where is Older Brother? Standing on the sideline, hoping against hope that he too may get the chance to hold the baby. On the other hand, Older Brother may also decide that caring for babies is "women's work."

When you are feeding or bathing the new baby, let your toddler son join in. Allow him to wash his own baby doll. Let him follow your actions and compliment him for doing a fine job. When he grows up he will be ready to handle the real event.

Males who are exposed to infants and take an active part in parenting are less likely to abuse children. (Herman, Judith Lewis, *Father-Daughter Incest*, Cambridge, Mass.; Harvard College Press, 1981).

Choosing a Doll

As practical, down-to-earth parents we all know that when helping our child choose a doll, our say in the matter is directly influenced by the media. Which doll is popular this month? If the child wants a genuine Cabbage Patch Kid and we attempt to substitute it with a cheaper version, look out! Dolls represent real people. Children have power over their dolls, they can direct their behaviour. On the other hand, when they play with them, it is not uncommon to see them act out *their* roles and those of other people.

When buying a doll, avoid the kind that depicts stereotyped sexist values — the Glamour Girl, the Macho Guy.

The most suitable dolls are those of appropriate size (not larger than the child). They should be washable, huggable and wear removable clothing. Acquiring an anatomically correct doll is an excellent idea, if you can find one.

If your child has more than one doll, you may want to add an ethnic or national one. It will help him adjust to life in a multi-racial society.

During the height of the Cabbage Patch Doll craze I spoke with a retailer about the phenomenon. She told me that if she could get more stock, she could sell thousands of these squashed-face creatures. Behind her, on a shelf, were several black Cabbage Patch Kids. "What about those?" I asked. "Oh, I just cannot sell them here," she said with regret. "This is a white neighbourhood. One mother told me yesterday she would like to buy one but her husband wouldn't have one in the home."

Why do we persist in damning our children to a lifetime of bigotry? That too is abuse.

Expected Behaviour

What are our objectives when we are attempting to rid our households, if not our lives, of sexist behaviour? Are we trying to make our boys into girls? Do we want our daughters to assume male characteristics? Definitely not. What we are searching for is androgyny — a state which takes the best from both sexes. We want our daughters to be strong, caring and gentle and we want no less for our sons. What needs to be eliminated are the extremes: tough only boys and sweet only girls.

Children know what sex they are. They have discovered the biological difference between male and female by the time they are three. Here are some examples of how children know their expected behaviours and roles:

1. On the way home from the hospital, a female baby is dressed in a pink T-shirt, a boy in a blue one.

2. Mothers and grandparents pay more attention to the physical appearances of girls than those of boys.

3. Boys are taught to "work it out." Girls are rescued.

4. Parents and grandparents applaud assertive behaviour in boys. Girls are called unladylike for the same behaviour.

5. Female children who help out in the garden snipping the hedge or pulling weeds, usually are closely supervised. Boys are taught not to put their foot under the lawn mower, then are quickly left to their own devices.

6. Girls are supposed to *know* how to sort laundry. Boys are carefully taught and usually not trusted to wash anything other than whites.

7. If a boy improperly loads the dishwasher and breaks all the dishes, it becomes a good story to recount at the office party. If a girl does the same thing — no story.

8. Boys paint houses; girls do the trim.

Here are some creative suggestions to combat sexism:

- Ask your child, "What is a boy? What is a girl?" Talk about the biological differences.
- Make a girl doll and a boy doll out of Play-Doh. Include all the parts.
- Talk about the language we use to describe different professions:

Fireman	Firefighter
Policeman	Police Officer
Postman	Letter Carrier
Stewardess	Flight Attendant
Manpower	Human Power

Older children can play a similar game:

History	Herstory
Hurricane	Himicane
Herpes	Hispes (just kidding!)

Keep going. Of course, the purpose of this game is to have some fun around the dinner table or on a long drive. However, we do want to sensitize our children to the common words we use daily because language does express the attitudes and perceptions that ultimately guide our behaviour.

Getting Rid of Sexism

Here are some creative suggestions:

1. Dress your children in non-sexist playclothes. Talk about these clothes. "Sarah, this jogging set will be great for running." "Alice, I bet the knees in these jeans will make it past all the bases at least once." By making such simple, light-hearted comments, we are encouraging healthy behaviour.

2. Let your child see that Dad also can cry and show sympathy, and that Mom know how to take charge and show strength.

3. Sing with your child such wonderful songs as, "If you're happy and you know it . . ."

4. Most parents accept masturbation as a normal part of life and a healthy development of sexuality. A mother might say to her boy, "Randall, it's okay to touch yourself (give yourself pleasure, make yourself feel good, etc.); however Daddy and I would prefer if you did it in your bedroom where it is private." As a rule, our female children do not gain the same sort of encouragement and acceptance of masturbation. Little girls are *still* being told to save themselves for Prince Charming, the prevailing attitude being, "Your body is a commodity. Don't let anyone touch it and don't you touch it either." If we accepted masturbation and refused to utter such strange and archaic

phrases, would we encourage permissiveness? Hardly. Teaching our children to respect their bodies and value their sexuality would only make them into more aware and better-informed individuals.

IX

DRESSING CHILDREN

It is not uncommon to see an infant lie in his cot, a pair of double-seamed designer jeans constricting his movements. A toddler skipping through the mud in $35.00 linen pants and hand-made moccasins also is a familiar sight.

The retail clothing industry is quick to capitalize on the "guilt market" — parents who provide children with goods rather than giving of their time. Children's clothing has become a multi-million dollar industry and, admittedly, its products are pretty impressive — safari outfits and leisure suits and, of course, what child could do without a leather pant suit?

Dressing children is a pleasure, however, it is important that they have some say in choosing their clothes, not only to develop their own tastes, but also to increase their awareness of how clothes are perceived. Dress them in a manner appropriate for their ages, keeping in mind that things that are fashionable and fun to wear can be incorporated into a sensible wardrobe. Pity the child who wears grey skirts and Oxford shoes in a world of colour. The key is always balance and compromise. If fluorescent is in style, and you are not prepared to slap down $38.95 on a lime dress, try settling for lime socks.

Winter Clothes

Snowsuits and boots usually are the biggest clothing investment we make, sports equipment excluded. As protective parents, we tend to overclothe our children assuming that they feel the cold in the same way we do.

We zip our youngsters into snowsuits in which Mr. T. could not move. Their hats usually are woollen and pulled down over their ears. We might even snap on a pair of ear muffs. A scarf is wound and rewound to cover neck and forehead. Big mitts and new chunky moon boots complete the picture. "Now kid, go out and play! Have a good time!"

The kid cannot hear. He has no peripheral vision and if the scarf falls over his eyes he will cease to see altogether. He cannot run and because the scarf is wrapped around his mouth he cannot talk either. If his suit is a light colour, he will blend in nicely with the snowbank; if it is navy or brown, better not send him out after 3:00 p.m., because he cannot be seen.

Active, healthy children are quite hardy. Buy a light-weight snowsuit with a shell hood tucked into the collar. All the child still needs are leggings, a hat, mittens, and a small scarf tucked inside. Better yet, let him wear a turtle-neck sweater or a dicky front. Instead of buying huge cumbersome boots, try a pair of rubber-soled mukluks. A mother I know knits a sailor sweater per year, per child. They are made of Icelandic wool that has been treated with oil. Her children wear these sweaters and a set of yellow sailing shells with matching pants. They keep warm as toast, dry, and their clothes are fashionable too.

If you choose to go for the more formal snowsuit, attach a strip of fluorescent tape to the back. Or, for the more fashion-conscious child, some fluorescent piping could be added around the shoulders.

Swimsuits

There she goes, three-year-old Rebecca, wearing her bikini. "Doesn't she look cute. My, she is getting a bad burn, though." Eight-year-old Alana looks even cuter in her bikini. "Just look at that walk. Kids sure are growing up fast, aren't they?"

Bathing suits on infants are for a purpose and if you doubt that, imagine fishing out "dump" (yes, we call it dump,) from the swimming pool. Bathing suits on toddlers and older children are worn to preserve developing modesty and a sense of privacy, as well as to prevent sunburn. The time will come when your nine-year-old daughter will demand a bikini. Making such things a bone of contention is not conducive to a good relationship with her. Point out that *Vogue* models usually are in one-piece bathing suits. If she is sports-minded, a preview of Olympic swimmers might stave off her request, for a while anyway.

Shoes are for Walking

Not long ago, I saw an eleven-year-old limping along in a pair of triple A ankle-high boots. The fact that she had double-

C-width feet did not deter her fashion-conscious self. On the other hand, it is not unusual to see a six-year-old playing in the park, shod with black patent leather shoes, making the climb up the slide steps as perilous as scaling the Matterhorn. Flat rubber bottoms is what we are after. Children's shoes should be comfortable and practical, conducive to a speedy get-away and healthy and safe playtime.

In summer, most children wear sandals. Let your small child walk around the house in them for a few days before she goes outside; they take a little getting used to.

Accessories

Jewellery, expensive or cheap, does not belong on young children. If it is only perceived to be precious it puts the child at risk with other children, as well as with dumb thieves. Necklaces, long or short, with or without pendants, simply do not belong on children when they are out and about.

However, even a small child should wear a watch. They can be bought for as little as $3.00. Children should know when and why things happen — Sesame Street comes on at 10:30, lunch is at 12:30. Relate time to the sun, to the seasons, to the world we live in.

For sale, makeup for the junior miss — target ages, six to ten. Is it a surprise then, to find our eleven-year-old wearing full face makeup, applied without rhyme or reason? Should we be astonished at the precision with which a ten-year-old applies four coats of "Smartie Red" nail polish? She's been doing it for the past three years!

They set out for school, wearing earrings, makeup, and pants so tight that their future ability to reproduce is at risk. What are they looking for? Sex? Of course not. They are after acceptance by their peers, confirmation of their budding adulthood. We know that and yet their clothes, their looks, their behaviour is viewed as provocative.* A charged molester's common cry often is, "She asked for it."

*A. Daniel Yarmey, Ph.D., Guelph University, "Older and Younger Adult's Attributions of Responsibility Towards Rape Victims and Rapists," *Canadian Journal of Behavioural Science*, 1985.

Dr. Yarmey's paper documents the perceptions of "demure" victims and victim demeanor as being less blameworthy (by younger subjects) of assault than "provocatively dressed" victims of same circumstance assault.

What else happens to children when they are dressed to beat the band? Their behaviour alters and their walk changes. How easy is it to lumber down the street in running shoes? Walking in high heels is not so easy. Dressed like women, they must converse and behave like women. What are we doing to our children? Why must they adopt adult ways before they have assumed the rights of childhood?

Society's Children

In a society that demands total self-reliance of each individual, we want our children to be responsible for themselves. This will save us time and money. The sooner they learn to "behave themselves," the sooner they will grow up and be left to fend for themselves.

The "Me" generation, while wanting the love of children on the one hand, is hesitant to assume the responsibilities children bring. Notice how unwelcome they are in many North American restaurants, sports clubs, apartment buildings.

It is fashionable to be pregnant but not to give birth. It is alright for a "hip" Mom to tote her infant on her chest as long as "it" does not do anything, such as cry or wet. Here is an often heard statement:

At the sports' club: "I pay my dues. I don't have kids. I don't like kids. They should not be allowed in. This place should be for adults only."

Each of us — parents, senior citizens, those who choose not to have children — must assume the responsibilities of our society. Children need us. Look at it this way: one day *they* will be paying our old age pensions!

X

STREET SMARTS

Small children should be rewarded for obeying the stop signs, diligently looking both ways before they cross the street, for telling everyone in the car to buckle up. Buy a role of big red dots or shiny gold "safety" stickers and keep them in your wallet. Peel off one when the occasion arises and stick it on your child's shirt.

The smallest child in your family may be assigned the duty of reminding everyone in the car to buckle up and to look both ways when crossing the street. If your two-and-a-half-year-old has performed the task well for a week or so, bestow on him the special title of "Safety Kid." However, do not be tempted to make a small child responsible for the safety of others.

The Bicycle

Would we, without providing driving lessons hand over a car to a sixteen-year-old and tell her to be careful? No, we would not. Why then, do we give an untrained child a bike and set him loose on an unsuspecting world?

Example:

"I was driving down our suburban street when a child of seven on a very large bike, cut in front of me. I was not going fast. I swerved and rammed the sidewalk. The child couldn't stop and crashed into my car. She was unhurt, thank God.

I told the little girl to sit on the grass while I went to get her mother who was in the back of the house. Her father was in the basement. They tore out, checked out their child and started yelling at me!

"The damage to my car was $1,100.00. I thought I would have to pay for it. About a month later, I got a bill in the mail for the cost of a new bike! We ended up going to court. I was as frightened as I was angry. I kept thinking, how come you people aren't happy that your child is alive?

"The judge made mincemeat of the parents. He asked them how come a seven-year-old was allowed to drive a brand-new bike on a road all by herself.

"Afterwards, I kept thinking, what if I had killed that child? I would have blamed myself for the rest of my life and yet I did everything right. People always feel sorry for the parents of a child who has been killed or badly hurt. I feel sorry for the driver, too."

Letting a child and his bike on the streets without safety training should be a crime.

Take your child to one of the police's road safety days *before* you give him his first two-wheeler.

A bike is not a toy. The attitude you have when giving your child her first bike should reflect the seriousness of the gift she receives and the responsibility that goes with it.

First bikes should never be state of the art. Choose one that is sensible and practical. It should have all the necessary safety features — a headlight and reflectors.

Periodically, check out the bike yourself. While you do want the child to be responsible for it you should not rely on her to tell you when the headlight battery has run down or the air in the tires is down.

Select a bike that is the right size for your child's height.

Why do boys' bikes have bars across the top and girls' bikes slanted bars? There is a structural reason why racing bikes have bars across the top. It is, however, unlikely that an average eight-year-old will participate in a high-speed rally.

Dirt/BMX bikes are now popular. They are unisex and designed to suit any child's height and weight.

Take the time to find the right bike for your child. Consult consumer reports. Select three or four types in your price range but allow her to make the final decision. If the bike is a hand-me-down, before repainting, let him choose the colour.

Under no circumstances, allow a child to wear a Walkman while riding a bike.

Spend a lot of time on the road with your child. Teach him the rules.

Example:

"Each of our children had to pass a road test and an oral examination before they were allowed to ride their bikes on the street. I once spotted my youngest son going through a stop sign. He lost the privilege of riding his bike for a week."

The Importance of Car Seats

Many parents believe that the safest way to transport a small child by car is in their arms. They are certain that before an accident occurs, they will have enough time and strength to protect him from injury. *That is not true.* For a child, the most dangerous place in the car is on the lap or in the arms of an adult.

In a series of tests conducted at the Highway Safety Research Institute in Michigan, male and female adult volunteers were safely fastened to their seats with lap and shoulder belts. Each volunteer held a 17-pound dummy which represented the size and weight of a six-month-old baby. They were then subjected to simulated 15 and 30 m.p.h. impacts. Not one of the volunteers was able to hold onto the "baby." Even knowing the precise moment of impact and using all their strength, they could not prevent the baby from being ripped from their arms and slammed into the dashboard.

Traffic accidents kills, maim, and permanently disable children. We have the power to change this. Put them in car seats, booster seats, and fasten their seat belts.

I once wanted to find out why parents do not buckle up their kids. Trying my best not to be or condescending, I walked up to cars, tapped on windows and asked politely, "Excuse me, I'm doing a survey on parents who do not put seat belts on their kids. How come your child is not wearing a seat belt?" I probably could have been a little more diplomatic but this job deserved danger pay. I was yelled at and told to mind my own #*+&! business! One charming fellow tried to hit me with his car door, another threatened to run me over. On the whole, however, I was ignored.

Here are some of the nicer responses I received from parents who had chosen not to buckle up their kids:

"My child just won't stay in a car seat."

"I'm a very careful driver."

"I'm only going a short distance."

"It takes too long to buckle them in."

"I've never had an accident."

"We didn't have car seats when I was young and I'm OK."

A former candy striper once told me her experiences in the children's ward of a large city hospital:

". . . I lasted one long day. The accidents I saw were beyond comprehension — a little girl with no fingers; she had fallen down an old-fashioned escalator; a little girl who had lost half her head when her braid had got caught on a roller coaster . . . and then, there was the little boy who had lost the bottom half of his face when the driver of the car he was in slammed on the brakes. The child was rammed into the dashboard. There was no accident. The car had simply stopped. One minute he was a normal kid, the next a cripple for life. He would never be able to talk or eat. He had twenty or so reconstruction operations ahead of him. He was four years old . . .!"

We have all seen people who sit children on their laps and let them "drive," those who put toddler in car seats but do not strap them in, drivers who let pre-teens sit in an open trunk, and parents who buy hundreds of dollars worth of protective hockey equipment but cannot stretch the budget far enough to pay for car seats.

When it comes to the safety of small children, I believe we *are* our brothers' keepers. At the risk of being responsible for hundred of black eyes, I charge you, the reader, with the task of saying something to all those who allow their children to flap around unrestrained on the insides of cars.

Buying a Car Seat

- Infants fare better in infant bucket seats. Do not buy toddler seats for them. Infant seats usually can be borrowed or rented. Check your local community service bureau or children's hospital and ask for further information.
- Toddler seats should be anchored at the top and the child

should be restrained at the bottom, usually by the adult seat belt.

- Look at the straps of the car seat. Are they complicated? Do they have extra attachments that could easily be lost?
- Check the width of the car seat. Some models are narrow and might not accommodate a child wearing a bulky snowsuit.
- Are the instructions easy to follow?
- Are the straps easily adjusted?
- Is it possible for a toddler to release herself from the seat while you are driving?
- Will the car seat fit your car?
- If the car seat you are using has been in an accident, check it for weak spots. Some individuals insist that car seats that have been in collisions or are otherwise damaged should be replaced.
- Do not substitute home feeding chairs for car seats.
- The National Child Passenger Safety Association in the United States believes that 80 per cent of child restraint seats are used incorrectly. Use car seats and use them properly.

Now, one critical element to a safe drive is that you yourself are belted. Show respect for your car and the road. Car seats are a relatively new addition to safe motor travel. We do not yet know whether children who were buckled in at a young age and are shown responsible motorist behaviour, will become safe or safer drivers. The odds are they will.

Note: The American Academy of Pediatrics, 141 Northwest Point Road, Elk Grove Village, Ill. 60007, has a list of recommended car seats and other pertinent information.

XI

BULLIES

Mention the word "bully" to a group of parents and they physically recoil. "Give me the measles, give me the mumps, but spare me the bully," is the usual comment. While many of us view bullies as part and parcel of childhood, most of us don't have the faintest idea how to handle a scenario in which they appear. As a result, we tend to ignore the predicament entirely, hiding behind such excuses as, "My son might as well learn that I cannot fight his battles for him," or, "She just will have to stand up for herself," and "Leave them alone; they will work it out." The most frequent remark is, of course, "If I step in, it will make matters worse."

A child who is being bullied feels threatened, frightened, and intimidated. If the situation is serious, as defined by the child, not by the parent, how can we make matters worse?

Imagine telling a small shop owner to be tough and stand up to the local hoods. Would it be right to recommend that the person being blackmailed seek legal or police aid? Of course! Why should *we* avail ourselves of outside resources to combat unacceptable behaviour while we leave our children to their own unsophisticated devices?

The abuse — verbal or physical — someone must take from a bully is very painful. Do not minimize it by calling it "just child's play." A bullied child who has been left to handle it on her own cannot see a way out of the situation. From the victim's perspective the only salvation is either to withdraw (into the house, into a shell) or to beat the bully at her own game. Either option is unacceptable. If the bully has a gang behind her, the situation usually seems hopeless. Once a child perceives herself as the victim she inevitably will assume some classic characteristics: become withdrawn, timid, dependent, easily spooked. In other words, at risk.

Do we want to fight all of our child's battles. No. If these battles must be fought and the opponents are of equal stature and age, our intervention should be minimal.

A true-blue bully does not involve himself in equal battles. If he knows that the parents of his victims are not behind them, his power and control increases considerably.

We want our children to be liked and accepted by their peers, and can minimize hostile actions by saying, "Alison, you are exaggerating. That girl doesn't hate you. She is just showing off. Ignore her." But will such reasoning help anyone even if our bully is showing off?

You may remember the time when your child was excluded from a sports event or not invited to a birthday party. As parents, we become angry, however, instead of helping our child overcome the hurt, we often find ourselves saying, "It doesn't matter, dear. That girl is just dumb. When *you* have a party, we won't invite her." Such a suggestion encourages hurtful, vengeful, and bully-type tactics. Surely, that was not our intent.

Children will be hard pressed to admit they are the target of another child's terrorizing tactics. It is embarrassing. Seldom will they come and tell us outright what is happening to them. In that respect, they are similar to the sexually molested child who fears a myriad of emotions, some of them shame and a desire for retribution. The bullied child dreads the label of coward or sissy. Innuendoes and behavioural changes can tip us off. Children may, for example, come home from school and refuse to return outside to play; they may develop stomach aches or cramps. In part, these physical ailments might be a ruse to avoid going to school altogether, or they may be psychological in nature. You may find small objects missing from the house or receive frequent requests for money. If you were to question the child about these objects or ask why she needs the extra money she may well take an offensive or defensive position, appear panic-stricken, etc. An independent child suddenly might become dependant. He might jump when the phone rings, repeatedly miss the school bus, lose his gym clothes, his lunch money or his lunch. The more obvious signs are bloody noses and unexplained or overexplained bruises.

Unless things are terribly wrong, we should try not to interfere until our child tells us about the incidents. However, this does not mean that we should sit back and do nothing. We may try playing the "What If" game or perhaps recant a tale from your own past. Finally, a child can be told, point-blank, that should a problem with a bully ever arise, you want to know about it.

When your child tells you about it, or you find out from another source and decide that this is serious stuff, sit down with him and outline together what the two of you can do. Take out a sheet of paper and write down all the suggestions. Pad your sentences. Even if your child does not yet read well, she will benefit from seeing the different avenues open to her. This gesture alone might give her enough courage to take a stand, providing the situation is not yet out of control.

A bully will pick on children who are either alone, i.e. temporarily without friends, or loners with no friends. By sitting down with your child and declaring your loyalty, you can remove this type of alienation. Above all things, the child must be lovingly told that he is not a coward or a sissy. A boy would benefit immeasurably from hearing his father state this. Remember, we are talking about children under ten here. Certainly, we don't want them to carry the heavy stigma of cowardice on their shoulders.

Consider steps the two of you can take. Not every suggestion will be applicable, however, by talking over some of the more overt ones, you may come up with a more subtle approach. Ask your child what she thinks, then devise a joint course of action:

1. If the bullying incidents take place in the classroom, call the teacher and alert her to the problem. Chances are your child's schoolwork is suffering. The teacher may even add some suggestions and insights into the situation.

2. If the bully is not a classmate but rather a schoolmate, consider calling the principal. In all likelihood, this particular child (the bully) is well known to the office. Remember, you only have heard your child's viewpoint, and while it is imperative that you believe him, you should become familiar with the overall problem.

3. You may want to request a meeting with the principal, the bully, a parent of the bully, yourself, and your child. Consider asking your child to leave the room with the bully to talk over the problem. Give them fifteen minutes to work things out. If they don't come up with an answer, tell them the adults will.

Why is this suggestion so important? First of all, it is difficult to continue bullying someone you know, and while it is unlikely that bully and victim will ever become friends, a bond will spring up between them if they are both made responsible for finding a solution. Instead of one against the other, the script has changed to kids versus adults.

"They tend to be people we like and trust, and their obvious and genuine care for children earns them our admiration. This, in part, explains why it is so very difficult for us to accept how badly we misjudge someone when he or she is discovered and how difficult it is for our children to tell us what happened."

The Safe Child Book,
Sherryll Kerns Kraizer

Secondly, a bully's tendency is to cast himself in the role of tough guy while the victim sees himself as the martyr. If we can break down these stereotypes, there is a good chance of settling the dispute.

4. If the trouble occurs on the street and not in the schoolyard, you might try talking to the bully. Don't act too authoratively or condescendingly. There are reasons why a child becomes a bully; using bullying tactics will only add to the problem. If your child continues to be harassed because of your action, take the next step.

5. Call the bully's parents. This is difficult for all parties concerned. State your case over the phone, adding that there are two sides to every story. Ask to get together with the parents in an attempt to work things out.

In all likelihood, the entire matter will dissipate. You probably will receive a call back telling you everything is OK. When it comes to actual confirmation, the parent of the abused child frequently becomes the arbitrator, and while it is necessary for someone to fill the role, do not make it look as if you had deserted your child. Also, try not to go overboard with accusations. A cool head is needed. Let everyone talk. As soon as possible, withdraw from the scene and let the children get on with it as best they can.

6. If the bullied child is a boy it usually is best to have a male intercede on his behalf. Sexist? Undoubtedly. We are trying to be practical here, and a father talking to another father with two young sons nearby will have more effect than a mother talking to another mother or a father.

I stress again, we must take action if circumstances suggest more than a childish tiff. Every year, we read about incidents were a child is tied to a tree and beaten; where a dare results in death.

I have not dealt with the makeup or the rehabilitation of a bully. After a great deal of thought, I came to the conclusion that if a child shows prolonged, hostile behaviour, professional guidance must be sought.

XII

MAKING FRIENDS

Children need friends, not only for protection but to develop their own self-concepts. How can we, as parents, encourage their friendships?

For our very young child, two or three years old, for example, we can initiate a friendship by making time and space available for it to develop. Join a toddler gym class and invite a few Moms over to your home. Small children do make "best" friends easily.

Encourage your toddler to make friends. This can be done by helping her introduce herself to a group of children while they are playing in the sandbox. Withdraw from the immediate scene as soon as possible, and watch from the sidelines.

Rejection is part of forming a friendship. Some overtures work while others don't. Rejection hurts and telling your child, "Oh, she wasn't good enough for you, anyway," is counterproductive. Never, ever make fun of your child's choice of friends. This is a particularly bad habit, often practised by parents of teenagers.

Children like to dress and look like one another. Pity the child who is forced to have a short haircut while his peers wear their hair long, or vice versa.

Children of ambitious parents also have a cross to bear. Some are pushed into becoming leaders against their will. It is not good enough that daughter is on the basketball team, she has to be the captain as well. Not only can this sort of thing do immeasurable damage to a child, but it could make her very unpopular with her peers. The best leaders are those who also are excellent team players.

Encourage your child to bring home friends. Invite the child's mother, at least for the first time. If that is not practical, call her up and have a chat over the phone. As a matter of principle, do not allow your child to play in someone else's home without having met the parents of the friend.

Friends protect each other from assault — not always but

most of the time. A child in a group is less likely to be singled out for molestation or abduction. Children who communicate easily and happily with their peers are less likely to tolerate the overtures of a molester. They have no need to comply with someone who offers sex under the guise of friendship.

XIII

ABUSERS

"They tend to be people we like and trust, and their obvious and genuine care for children earns them our admiration. This, in part, explains why it is so very difficult for us to accept how badly we misjudge someone when he or she is discovered and how difficult it is for our children to tell us what happened."

The Safe Child Book,
Sherryll Kerns Kraizer

What does an abuser look like? He has inordinately long black teeth, hair growing out of the palms of his hands, and he has yellow, beady eyes and lives under a rock. The truth of the matter is — abusers are ordinary people, they look just like us. As difficult as this is to comprehend, there is no sure-fired way of identifying them.

Below are some observations about abusers. I list them with dread. Will you assume that an individual who does not fall into one of the specific categories, could not, would not abuse a child? I repeat, we must scrutinize all people who deal directly or indirectly with our children. We remain their protectors.

- Take caution when your child is involved (through school, sports, etc.) with an adult who spends all of his/her waking hours in the company of children. An individual who teaches school, runs a cub scout pack, coaches hockey, teaches Sunday School does not have much time left to enjoy adult pursuits.

It would be ridiculous to suggest that *all* adults who spend *all* their time with children must be abusers. However, you have to stand back and ask yourself why an adult would spend the major portion of his/her time solely in the company of children.

- Take caution when an individual makes continual references to children in a sexual manner. ("Boy, look at that little knock-out.")

Most of us have said about a little girl, "When she grows up, she is going to break a lot of hearts." Proud Grandpas usually voice such sentiments. However, there is a difference in tone between that and referring to children as sex objects. Listen carefully, you will feel the difference.

- Beware of individuals who were sexually or physically abused as children.

Example:

"I knew this friend of mine for years. Brenda had a bad childhood, really bad. Raised by strict authoritarians, she had suffered emotional and some physical abuse. We live in different cities now.

"A year or so ago, she came to stay with us for a week, but it seemed like a month. From the moment she entered our home, she seemed to spend most of her time being annoyed by my two-year-old daughter. She bossed her and even tried to send her to bed because the child was "fooling around" with the T.V. dials. It came to a head when she told my daughter to carry a full litre of milk to the fridge. Well, my daughter tried. Just as she reached the fridge, the carton slipped out of her grasp and fell to the floor. I smiled and got up to clean it. Before I was out of the chair, Brenda stood over her, yelling. She called her clumsy and again told her to go to her room. I picked up my daughter and took her to my bedroom.

"I then had to ask Brenda to leave. What a scene! I love this woman, but just couldn't allow her to abuse my daughter this way. The hardest part was, I felt I was penalizing her for her childhood. She couldn't help the way she was brought up."

What if we do meet individuals who had a difficult childhood, do we label them as abusers and exclude them from our lives? What a horrible thought! Let us watch the behaviour of adult and child together. If we don't like what we see, it is best to meet outside our house.

- Take caution with adults raised with strict authoritarian

rules who remain remote from the society of children, yet feel compelled to direct their behaviour.

We all know childless individuals who like to tell us, "If that were my child, I'd . . ." Take care not to leave your child with persons who have very definite ideas about "correct" childhood behaviour. They may not become sexually or physically abusive, but their attitudes would be detrimental to encouraging your child's self-esteem.

• Beware of individuals who drink heavily and frequently.

Many illegal acts — drunken driving and sexual assault — are committed while under the influence of alcohol. The excuse, "I was drunk and didn't know what I was doing," is *never* acceptable.

• Beware of volatile individuals with violent tempers who make a practice of venting their anger on people or objects around them.

Individuals who cruelly kick a dog or worse, beat their spouses, are not people we want around our children. We all know that talking in generalities is a dangerous practice, however, individuals who berate other people in public and derive satisfaction from belittling them, might well be tipping us off to other problems.

• Take caution — abusers are devious individuals. They may work hard to establish themselves as fine, upstanding persons. They may make friends with many children but molest only one. Not only will a shy child have trouble speaking, but the other children may serve as character witnesses for the abuser.

We often read about a sexual abuser who is a nice man and lives around the corner with his wife and three kids. Abusers fall into three categories:

1. *Fixed or Fixated Offenders*

The fixated offender staggers helplessly through life. He

may by married, but usually there is an adult nearby to help him survive the day-to-day trials. He is a person who, from a young age, has been sexually attracted to young children even though he might have other sexual experiences. He is immature and seeks camaraderie and companionship from children. He perceives his victims as the motivators to the act: "She started it." "He was asking for it." "If she didn't want it, why did she walk out of the bathroom nude?"

The average fixated offender is between 27 and 29 years of age.

2 . Regressed Offenders

These are individuals who originally may have preferred their peers as sexual partners, but once the stress of adulthood set in, they looked to children for compensation and reinstatement of control and power. Seventy-five per cent of these offenders are married and range in age between 32 and 36 years.

3 . Adolescent Offender

"Perhaps more than any other category of child molesters, we must be careful when defining the adolescent offender. He or she is a person in teen years who molests children. However, the adolescent offender usually has not had enough varied sexual experience to choose child molesting as the preferred sexual expression. Rather, the offences are reflections of a disturbed state of his life at that time." (Sandford, Linda T., *The Silent Children*, McGraw-Hill Book Co., 1980).

The adolescent offender seldom uses violence to seduce or molest his victims. Normally, the molestation will take place under the guise of a game, such as strip poker, by utilizing such normal practices as giving children a bath, or helping them on and off with their clothes. Most adolescent offenders do not use force nor do they necessarily attempt to penetrate a child. Molestation will be through masturbation, exhibition, etc.

Strangers

There are valid reasons for believing that if a person were to harm our child, it would be a stranger.

- We don't want to admit that anyone within our small world would deliberately hurt our child.
- If a stranger molests our child, we can rely on the excuse of chance: We were in no way responsible for bringing the molester into our child's world.
- Strange or violent crimes are publicized in the media. We hear about them but not about those committed by known abusers. Crimes by known abusers are not as likely to be reported.
- We feel comfortable stereotyping a stranger — old, dirty looking, degenerate. We cannot apply the same adjectives to an abuser who is known to the child.

There are two types of stranger offenders — the sadist who uses excessive violence for his own ends, and the individual who only uses violence if he "feels" it is necessary.

The minds of these offenders remain remote to us. While many individuals experience some sort of sexual fantasies involving children, only a select few will act them out. Various elements must be in place before someone molests a child. To find a way to rationalize the act, the offender must have access to children and be motivated and able to overcome all inhibitions. Abusers usually suffer from low self-esteem, inability to cope with the adult world, and from an extreme lack of parenting skills. Those who have been abused themselves, consciously or unconsciously, seek to vent their anger, fear, and frustration on a child.

At the risk of sounding repetitious: *Stereotyping offenders is a dangerous practice.*

Children at Risk

Some children may be more at risk than others, however, if our child does not fit into the following list, does that mean we can sit back and relax? Obviously not. In general terms, at risk are:

- Children who are left unattended for part of the day, i.e. latchkey kids.
- Children who appear unkempt. They may have bad teeth, torn clothing, and be dirty in appearance.
- Children who find themselves separated from their peers. i.e. children with handicaps, those who are new to the neighbourhood, and loners.
- Children who are undergoing stress, i.e. those who experience such home difficulties as divorce or a parent's unemployment. Also children who have difficulties in school or are under pressure from a bully.
- Children who seldom are seen with a parent or guardian, i.e. those who continually turn up at sports or social events without an adult.
- Foster kids or those who live in and out of all sorts of homes, seemingly in the care of no one.
- Children who are seen smoking at a young age or repeatedly hang out at shopping centres or arcades.
- Children who are ignorant about sex or sexual acts.
- Children who live under strict authoritarian rules in families with communications problems.
- Children who do not know whether they are loved and valued.

Is that to suggest that our bright, beautiful child with straight teeth, vigilant, caring parents, who does not hang around arcades, knows about sex, lives in an open and communicative home, is not at risk? No, no, no! It is harder, however, to strike up a relationship with a child who must account for her time and is aware of proper and expected adult behaviour.

XIV

THE TOOLS OF THE MOLESTER

What does a molester offer a child? Why do children make return visits to an offender? In so many cases, why does the child not tell?

Bribery, flattery, friendship, coersion, and threats are the favourite tools of a molester. Consider the following two fictitious stories:

Sarah's Artist Friend

It was summer. Sarah had just moved into a new neighbourhood. She was very shy and had yet to meet new friends. If only she could move back home again. She missed the club house, her Brownie pack but, most of all, her best friend Amanda. Dad had been transferred here and was working hard in his new office. Mom was busy decorating their new home and taking care of the baby. Sarah didn't like the new baby very much. Things just seemed to go wrong for her since his arrival.

Sarah was eight years old. One day, she was walking down the street. She saw a man mowing his lawn. He waved but Sarah pretended not to see him. The next day, he called out to her, "Nice day, isn't it?" Sarah nodded and ran away. After that, she often stopped to talk to the man. She would hang over his fence, put her feet on the bottom plank and sway.

He said his name was Brian. She wondered why he wasn't at work like her Dad, but then she remembered that Amanda's Dad didn't go to an office either. He was a writer and worked at home. Maybe Brian was a writer too? One day she asked him what he did to make money. He laughed and told her to come inside. Sarah walked into the house and gasped! Paintings were propped up against the wall, against each other and there even was paint on the floor! Her Mom wouldn't like this place at all. Brian showed Sarah all sorts of neat things. He made her a cup of tea and the two of them sat down on the floor to drink it. Sarah felt very grown up. Maybe this new neighbourhood wasn't so bad after all?

Sarah went home and told her Mom that she had a new friend. His name was Brian. Mom looked relieved and said it was good Sarah was finally making some friends.

The next day Sarah ran out of the house extra early. She wanted to see Brian again. When she got there, he was not yet dressed. He answered the door in his robe. He looked funny; his hair was sticking out all over the place. Brian told Sarah to wait in the kitchen while he got changed. Then he made a pot of tea and, this time, they sat down at the kitchen table. Sarah really didn't like the taste of tea but she thought drinking it was a very grown-up thing to do.

Brian asked Sarah about her old house, about Amanda, about her old school. Sarah told him everything. It was good to tell someone how she felt. He said he knew what it was like to come to a new town. When was little, his family had moved around a lot, too.

Suddenly, Brian snapped his fingers and jumped out of the chair. He said he had a great idea! Why doesn't he paint a picture of Sarah! After all, wasn't she the prettiest girl in the world? Sarah laughed. She wasn't all that pretty but was glad Brian thought so.

Brian rushed into the livingroom or the painting room, as he called it. He started pulling pictures off the shelves. Sarah walked over to look at them. They were photographs of young girls but they didn't have any clothes on! Brian kept pulling out more pictures of naked children. He said this was true art. Sarah nodded knowingly.

Finally, Brian told her where to stand and to take off her clothes. Sarah felt funny but Brian said that one day her picture would be in a really big art gallery. Sarah didn't know what an art gallery was but she told him she had once been to a museum. "Same thing," Brian said. Sarah shyly took off her clothes.

Over the next few weeks, Brian made lots of pictures of Sarah. He told her not to tell her Mom about them because it would spoil the surprise. Sooner or later, she could give them to her parents. It would make them proud of her.

One day while Sarah was posing, Brian sat down next to her on the sofa and began stroking her chest. She was suddenly afraid but his voice calmed her down. He said she was a big girl now, and if she would let him touch her, she would be his girlfriend and he her boyfriend. Not even Amanda had a boyfriend!

The next day, the same thing happened, except that Brian showed her what a man looked like. He opened his robe. Sarah jumped back and almost screamed. Brian just laughed and asked her to touch him. Sarah said no. Suddenly, he got very angry and yelled at her. He said that she wasn't a big girl after all. She was a stupid, little girl and could leave immediately. Sarah didn't want to go. She didn't have any other friends. What if Brian didn't talk to her anymore? Shyly, Sarah walked over to him and said she was sorry. She would do what he wanted her to do. Brian smiled and said that he had been wrong; she really was a big girl.

That night, Sarah asked her Mom about touching and stuff. Her Mom asked her what she meant. Sarah didn't know. Then she asked what Mom and Dad did at night. Her mother frowned and asked her to be more specific. Finally, Sarah asked her where babies came from. Amanda had once told her they came from people touching each other. Sarah's Mom looked startled. She said she would tell Sarah about it when she was older. She was too young to hear about that sort of thing now.

The Child Sexual Abuse Syndrome — repeated abuse of a child as willing accomplice — is new to the language of sexual offence. Why do children return to "the scene of the crime," why do they allow themselves to be abused? Because the abuser often fulfills their emotional needs.

Sarah was without friends. She lacked parental guidance and communication. Would Sarah have complied with the offender in her old neighbourhood? Not likely.

Here is another story:

Teacher's Pet

Alex had turned seven the day he entered his fourth foster home. He was small for his age and most people thought he was much younger. The house he was to live in was filled with lots of little kids. Mrs. Mason had three children of her own plus two other foster kids. Alex shared a room with Christopher, Mrs. Mason's oldest son. Up until then Christopher had had the bedroom to himself. He hated Alex on sight.

Alex's last three foster homes had been close to his old school. He would start at a new school the very next morning. He was scared. He wished he could go to his Mom's house, but the social worker said he couldn't, not until his Mom had "straightened out." His Mom was supposed to visit him every Sunday, but most of the time she forgot.

Alex's social worker's name was Bill. He had a long ugly beard and was skinny. Mom called him, "Billy Blue Beard." Bill once told Alex that his Mom had hurt him when he was little. She was sick and needed therapy to get better.

Alex hated Billy Blue Beard so much he could have spit at him. Once he did, but his Mom told him never to do that again because he could put Alex in a foster home forever.

School was awful. The kids were different from those in his old school. They were rich. A couple of them even had Walkmen.

Alex's new teacher's name was John Dier. All the kids called him "Mr. Tire" because he was fat around the middle. It was neat knowing a teacher's first name. For a long time, Alex thought teachers didn't have first names. Mr. Dier was nice to Alex. At recess he would call him up to his desk and ask him all sorts of questions. Alex started to tell him about his new foster home, his stupid roommate Christopher, things like that.

One day, Mr. Dier asked Alex to stay after school. He said he needed to do some extra work. At first Alex was mad but then he realized he didn't have anything better to do.

Alex stayed behind. Mr. Dier said he would help him with some assignments. After a while he asked Alex if he wanted to go get something to eat. Alex thought that was a neat idea. They couldn't leave the school together because it was against the rules for a teacher to take a student out to eat. If Alex could find his way to the *Rambling Rose Restaurant* Mr. Dier would meet him there.

A half hour later, they were eating delicious hamburgers. Mr. Dier told Alex he could call him Jim. Alex was confused; wasn't his name John? Mr. Dier said his best friends called him Jim. Imagine, having a teacher for a friend!

Jim walked Alex part of the way home. As they were passing a department store Alex spotted a Walkman in the window. He wanted one very badly. Jim went into the store and bought one for him. Just like that! Alex thought his new foster mother would ask him where he got it. He would tell her his mother gave it to him.

Alex stayed after school a lot. Mr. Dier sent a note to his foster mother telling her Alex needed extra lessons. Once in a while, they did some reading but mostly they went to restaurants and even to Jim's apartment.

Jim bought Alex lots of neat stuff but he wasn't allowed to bring any of it home. Jim said no one must find out about it because he would lose his job and never see Alex again. Alex promised never to tell.

One day Jim took Alex to a sports club. It was neat. They went swimming and then had a shower together. The next afternoon, Jim suggested they have a shower together in the apartment. Alex thought this was weird but then Jim brought out a brand-new ghetto blaster. He told Alex that he would have to start paying for some of these things. But Alex had no money. Jim said he could pay in another way. Alex sort of knew what he was talking about. Billy Blue Beard, the social worker, had once said something about touching. Alex looked around at all the neat stuff in the room. He thought of the sports club and he remembered Christopher, the Creep . . . If it was only a couple of times . . .

While most kids are not physically harmed by sexual assaults, some assaults lead to penetration. Alex was bribed into being a victim. Jim had no need to use force.

Remember the first time you saw a teacher of yours outside the school, perhaps in a food store? What a revelation it was to find out that teachers ate! By understanding that those in positions of authority also are human beings a child will be better protected from those who might abuse such positions.

Offenders consciously put their needs above those of the child. Just as children do not understand the consequences of abusive acts, neither do they feel they have the resources to seek help, even if they realize they are in trouble.

In both stories assault was gradual. This is typical of an offender.

Why Children do not Tell

If the molestation begins when a child is quite young, he may not realize for some time what is going on. As children approach their teens, they may well understand what is happening to them, and may begin to wonder why they hadn't stopped it earlier. They are ashamed and may blame themselves.

What if nobody believes them, especially if the abuser is a family member? They fear retribution.

The child may also feel she must continue to protect the offender, for fear he might suffer a terrible fate.

To reverse this logic, the child might feel that if she did tell, Dad would get so angry, he would kill the offender and then Dad would go to jail!

Children who do tell a parent but do not receive immediate response, may assume that the parent doesn't care. There are as many reasons why children don't tell, as there are victims of molestation.

Stranger Assaults

Contrary to public belief, most stranger assaults are not rape but exposure. Some children are "flashed" in the raincoat-fashion and think little of it. Others may be traumatized by the experience. Exposure may produce fear and mistrust in a child. For that reason such episodes must be reported to the police.

What parents fear most are rape or sudden life-threatening physical abuse. Statistically, such attacks are infrequent in comparison to gradual molestation by an offender who is known to the child. Violent attacks usually are reported to outside sources — doctors, psychologists, the police.

Should a sudden attack occur in our lives or in those of our children, we must try and put it into perspective. This may sound absurd but it is important to recognize the time frame in which such an attack took place. Given the total time we likely will spend on this earth, we must realize that minutes or even a few hours, should not and cannot irreparably damage an entire young life. Suffer, mourn, work, and heal. Seek the right professional helf for the entire family. Be confident that with unrelenting love and patience, child and family will recover.

Reporting Molestations

If your child tells you she has been molested, stay calm. She is safe now. Tell her so. "It will not happen to you again because Mommy and I are going to protect you. I know it is hard, but I want you to tell me as much as you can. Come close, and start at the beginning. I love you Debbie and I believe you."

Do not reach for the phone the moment your child starts to talk. It will take a while for the whole story to come out, perhaps even a few days or longer. Chances are, your child will give you only a little bit of information to begin with. Your initial reaction will be either to encourage her to go on, or to discourage her from saying anything further.

Do not change the child's words. While you may ask questions to clarify points, you must not substitute her words for your own. Nor is it advisable to allow anyone else to "coach" the child. Keep the child physically close. She will need some good touching to feel truly loved.

Depending on the area in which you live, contact the appropriate authorities — Children's Aid, the police. You also may want to get in touch with a local rape crisis centre to obtain information, legal advice, etc.

Reporting helps the child understand that sexual abuse of children is wrong and that the adult involved will be punished. Although our first concern is for the abused child, we cannot allow an offender to continue. By *not* reporting an abuse, we are, in essence, abandoning the child and cooperating with the offender. As individuals we can do little to stop further abuses unless we have support from the authorities.

XV

LISTEN TO YOUR CHILDREN

What words would a child use to let us know something has gone wrong? Do children, in fact, tell us they have been offended/molested but we fail to understand? How do we expect a child to inform us of the abuse?

Examples:

Child: "Mommy, he tickles me."
Mom: "You mean he tickles you and you laugh?"
Child: "No, I don't laugh."
Mom: "He tickles you on the neck and under your arms?"
Child: "No, he tickles me down there."

How about this one?

Child: "I hate my teacher."
Mom: "She must have done something really terrible to make you feel like that."
Child: "Yea, she moved my desk."

Are we trying to muckrake here? No. We simply want to understand what goes on in our children's lives. We want to interpret, not only their words but also the meaning of those words.

Perhaps, children think they have conveyed to us what happened and hearing no outcry or protest, they may believe the situation to be anything from "normal" to "their fault." They might say, "Mr. Potts isn't very nice", or "How come Mr. Bean wears weird underwear?" Such phrases need our attention. Children send out signals we either can pick up or ignore. Perhaps Mr. Potts told your daughter to get off his grass, and your son may have seen Mr. Bean's polka-dotted shorts hanging on the clothes line. On the other hand, perhaps not. It is up to us to ask the one extra question, "What do you mean by that?"

Children have a lot of ways to show us something has gone wrong. Here are a few:

— Not wanting to go with or stay with an individual.

— Having a lot of nightmares or developing an ab - normally high number of new fears.

— Becoming moody.

— Displaying nervous or hostile behaviour.

— Running away.

— Becoming provocative or sexually promiscuous.

— Withdrawing from peers or social relations.

— Showing regressive behaviour.

— Committing acts of aggression — petty theft, bullying, etc.

— Displaying personality changes — an outgoing child becomes clingy, withdrawn.

— Changing their toilet habits.

— Talking a lot about sex or displaying an exorbitant interest in their genitals. Making attempts to touch their parents' genitals.

— Having a diagnosed case of venereal disease or other problems related to penetration, such as soreness, bleeding, etc.

With the exception of the last point, all of the above are signs of a disturbance in a child's life but do not necessarily mean the child has been molested.

It is unlikely that molestation by an offender known to the child will take place suddenly or happen just once. The abuser may persue the child, much like a man courts a woman, or a woman courts a man. The offender who is known to child and family must first find out if his victim can be bribed, intimidated, or coerced. Will the child keep a secret? Are the parents in tune with the child?

Can molestation be stopped before it starts? Most of the time but not all of the time.

Children Who Tell

Who is the first, most likely person a child would tell about being sexually molested? Who would we first tell if something happened to us? Would we go to the police? No. Chances are we would tell a friend; children would follow the same pattern.

Example:

"I was driving in the car with my seven-year-old son when he came out with, 'Mommy, do you know what it is called when a man puts his penis in a little boy's bum?' I said I did not know. He replied, 'It's called piggy.'

"I let the matter drop but once home, sat down with him and asked him where he had heard about piggy. My son did not want to answer. He looked up at the light then down at his feet, he even tried to change the subject. It took twenty long minutes before I could join together all the bits and pieces.

"A schoolfriend of his, call him Rob, had told my son about how men pee on little boys and what it was like to have all your clothes taken off and thrown into a closet. The list went on.

"What should I do? I don't know the little boy. I don't know where he lives or who his parents are. But I do feel Rob is asking for help."

This mother had a difficult job to do. The law states we must report a suspected child abuse. No one wants to falsely accuse another of deviant behaviour. However, common sense must prevail; a seven-year-old could not have, would not have been able to make up the story. If it w as fabricated he easily could be unmasked by a trained psychiatrist or psychologist.

Keeping Secrets

Secrecy is the most important element of a successful molestation by a perpetrator known to the child. How can we explain to children about good and bad secrets? What is the difference between a surprise and a secret?

We may try to eliminate the word "secret" altogether, insinuating that all secrets are bad but that would not deal with phrases such as, "This is just between us," "This is our little game," "Nobody has to know," etc.

Children associate secrecy with games, whispering and playing jokes on people. All club rules include an oath of secrecy. If you break it, you'll "suffer a horrible death."

Secrecy is part of our children's inner world. They may revel in it or have trouble dealing with it. What can we say to them about secrets? Try this:

"Billy Joe, if another child told you to keep a bad or funny secret, I think you should tell me about it. Here is a funny secret: What if a friend of yours said, 'I have a bad stomach ache, don't tell anyone.' Would you tell me? Yes, you should tell me so I can help him. Big people should not tell little people to keep secrets. It's always OK if you tell me about the secrets big people ask you to keep."

A common retort to this last sentence is, "What if the secret is a surprise birthday party or something?" So what if a child tells you about it! Thank him and say, "I'm glad you told me. It's hard to understand the difference between a good secret and a bad one. This is a good secret. I'm glad you told me."

Other adults may counter your efforts to streetproof your children. A babysitter may offer various treats to bribe your child into behaving, a grandparent may tell him, "Your Mommy would be mad at me if she knew I was giving you candy, so let's not tell her, OK?"

The film *Strong Kids/Safe Kids* relates keeping a bad secret to having a splinter in your little finger. No one can see it and only you can feel it. A bad secret, like a splinter, hurts until someone removes it.

Who Owns your Body?

"God does," a six-year-old told me during a streetproofing workshop. "My parents," said another little girl. "I dunno," was the general response. "You do," I said. "Your body is your own and no one is supposed to hurt it or fool around with it in any way you don't like. *Your body belongs to you.*"

Continually, we sabotage our own efforts to establish this fact. While we tell children that they own their bodies, we physically show them that they do not. We come up from behind them, lift them up in the air, and laugh at the expression on their faces. We may go too far in a tickling session, wash them roughly or scrub their faces against their will.

Certainly, there are times when we have no choice but to pick up a child to remove him from the scene. A child throwing a tantrum is a case in point. On the other hand, we can warn her about the upcoming airlift. We can say, "Mommy needs this chair. I'm going to put you on the floor," or "I have to wash your face now. You're not going to like it, I know." If such statements sound foreign to you, all you need is a little practice.

What does one say to the child who believes God owns her body? We can explain that God has given us a body to take care of. We must brush our teeth and hair, keep our nails trimmed, and take showers. We must eat good food and exercise. Not allowing anyone to harm our bodies is just another way of taking care of ourselves. Many children truly believe that they do not own their bodies. Mom may put too much emphasis on toilet training or reprimand the child for masturbating.

As parents concerned about sexual molestation, we must make our children believe that no one must ever touch their private parts. That is why I object to such categorical statements as "No one is allowed to touch your private parts." It may be better to say, "People shouldn't put their hands down a little kid's pants" "When you are grown up and love someone you will want to take your clothes off." As always, our concern is balance and providing explanations with the right kind of words.

XVI

TALKING TO YOUR CHILDREN

Not long ago, while speaking to a class of concerned parents about streetproofing and sexual molestation, I posed the question, "What if parents made the conscious decision *not* to talk to their child about sexual molestation, protection, and streetproofing? What if that child were molested? Who's fault would it be?" After a few murmurs, the response came, "It would be the parents' fault. After all, they made a conscious decision and the child ultimately suffered for it." I then posed a second question: "What if parents had done their best to street-proof their child and the child *was* molested? Who's fault would it be now?" One response was, "Well, this is too hypothetical. What were the circumstances of the molestation?"

Before we can begin to talk to our children about abduction and sexual molestation — about abuse of all types — we must know these facts:

It is the molester's fault that the incident took place. Not the child's, not the parents', nor the teacher's, the babysitter's, or anyone else's fault. It does not matter that the child was acting "in a suggestive manner," whatever that may mean. Nor does it matter what a child was wearing, or under what special circumstances the molestation took place.

It is irrelevant that the child went along with the molestation or even claimed to "enjoy" the acts. Who cares whether or not the child previously was a "chaste character." Children do not know the implications of sexual acts. They are never, never at fault.

No one holds a gun to the head of a molester. He is not "egged on" by the child or peers and, while it is true that many adult offenders had been molested as children, as parents we must place the responsibility where it belongs. Abusers choose to abuse.

We cannot fully protect our children, of that we can all be sure. We can arm them with knowledge and we can talk to them. But how? When? How can we explain the tricks big people may play on little people? How does an adult tell a child about deviant behaviour? What words do we use to let him know that sometimes, just sometimes, nice people do bad things? These are difficult questions to answer. Often, the major stumbling block is not the researching of the topic or the paraphrasing of the words; it is confronting the idea that in our attempts to educate our children we are tainting their world. A further stumbling block is admitting to ourselves that yes, someone could hurt our child, maybe even someone we know and love.

Ask yourself, where is the best place to comfortably talk to my child? Are we both at ease while folding the laundry? Is there an activity we can share that is conducive to conversation?

When is the best time to talk? While sitting on the grass on a Saturday afternoon? (Avoid before bedtime, if possible. No child wants to hear about protection just before the lights go out). While it would be nice to find the perfect time and place, do not put too much emphasis on that. Often as not, if we are truly looking for the golden opportunity, we will find it. Grasp it and go for it. Perhaps you will say everything all wrong and find yourself talking to a potted plant while your child dozes off. No matter, keep trying.

What we want to avoid are syrupy phrases that sound condescending. Ask non-judgmental questions, such as, "Have you ever heard the word rape?" "What does a stranger look like?"

Tell your child the truth, tell her you are having a hard time dealing with the idea that someone might try to make her feel bad. Tell her that you do not want to frighten her, that it is unlikely that anyone would hurt her, but that you want to talk about it anyway. Relate talking about the subject to other types of protection. For instance, "It is not very likely that we will ever have a large house fire because we are very careful about matches and such, but we still have smoke detectors in our house and to go fire drills. This is called taking precautions. There are other kinds of precautions we can take . . ."

Keep trying. Your child will recognize your efforts and help you.

The "What If" Game

This game will benefit children and parents, from toddler-hood through the teenage years. One day, we may say to our sixteen-year-old daughter, "What if you were at a party with a guy and he started to drink a lot. Now suppose he insisted upon driving you home. What would you do?"

We can initiate our infants and toddlers to this game by asking our fifteen-months-old, "What if I dropped this raw egg on the floor, what would happen? Boom! That's right. It would smash." We might ask our two-year-olds, "What would happen if we left the roller skates on the stairs?" No response. "Someone might come down the stairs and trip. Maybe they would hurt themselves. Ouch! Let's put the skates in the closet." As a child's ability to speak increases, the game becomes more sophisticated. It should be a fun thing to do and play.

Here are some examples of What Ifs:

- What if you were really hungry and wanted a candy? Where could you get one?
- What would you do if you were playing with a truck and some other child came and took it away?
- What would you do if you smelled smoke in the house and everyone was asleep?
- What would you do if you came home and nobody was in?
- What would you do if you won a million dollars? What would you do with it?
- What would you do if the babysitter said you could stay up and watch TV until late if you didn't tell me she was smoking?
- What would you do if a friend fell off his bike and cut his leg really badly?
- What would you do if your best friend lived across the street and you were not allowed to cross the street?
- What would you do if the babysitter had a friend over and told you not to tell me?
- What if you were over at a friend's house and his Dad said, "Everyone in the car, we are going for a hot dog." What would you do?

- What would you do if someone said, "Your Mom is sick at the hospital, she had an accident. Come with me and I'll take you to her."
- What would you do if you found a lighter on the street?
- What would you do if you saw a wire hanging from a pole?
- What would you do if you wanted to cross a busy street and there was no one to help you?

Cover every topic under the sun and include some crazy What Ifs.

While we may want the questions to relate specifically to the child's environment, we also want them to be easily applied to similar circumstances. For example, we do *not* want to ask, "What if you were in the school washroom and a teacher walked in and made you take down your pants in front of him. What would you do?" There is a distinct possibility that having heard such a question, your child will avoid the school washroom for the rest of the year! Phrase the question in this manner, "What if you were by yourself and someone bigger than you told you to do something you did not want to do? What would you say to that person? What would you do?"

Keep in mind, there is never a right or a wrong answer, just a better one. To introduce the idea of expected and acceptable behaviour from adults, ask:

"What if you did something wrong, really wrong; can you think of something you should not do? What if you dug up some shrubs in the park? That would be wrong. Now, what if the park attendant came along and told you that unless you did as he said he would tell your parents about digging up the shrubs. What would you do?"

Now would be a good time to say, "No matter what you do, do not feel ashamed to come and tell me about it. When someone says, 'Unless you do as I say' they mean to harm you. We call that blackmail."

"What are some other things children do that are wrong?"

"What are some other things adults do that are wrong?"

At this stage of the game, you are well on your way to openly talking about matters that concern you both.

There is another reason why we want our children to have a "good feel" for the What If game. Sometimes it is difficult to talk about things that may be a little embarrassing, such as about being bullied, for example. Occasionally, children may be able to use the What If game as a vehicle to discuss them. Here are two examples:

"Mom, what if the teacher said you could be class monitor and then left the room, and a big guy in the back of the class said if you squealed on him 'cause he was talking he would beat you up? What would you do?"

A mother of a ten-year-old told me this one:

"Mom, what would you do if you wanted to French-kiss, and didn't know how?"

By not judging nor zealously correcting or condemning our children, we will provide them with an opportunity to talk with us. Where once they might have kept their thoughts hidden or their problems a secret, they may now have found a way to voice to us their inner feelings and concerns.

XVII

USING THE WORLD AROUND US

By the time most children reach the advanced age of five, they will have seen some 250,000 television commercials.* Children know their commercials, in fact, many seem to prefer them to the shows!

We can use the media, first, to further our children's abilities to make judgments; second, to help explain "tricks" to them and third, to teach them to understand what advertising is all about. We want our children to become discerning consumers.

In the context of streetproofing here is an idea, using television commercials, that helped me explain "tricks people play" to children between five and eight. The premise is to talk about tricks in a way that will not be the least bit frightening. We, therefore, use a medium that is both familiar and unthreatening to them.

Three little friends helped me out with my original experiment; a seven-year-old boy, a six-year-old girl, and a five-and-a-half-year old girl. While we were watching television a familiar orange juice commercial came up. As it happened, I had that exact same brand in my freezer. I asked the children:

Sharon: Do you think that orange juice is really as good as that person said it was?
Children: I dunno. Sure. Is the Smurfs coming on now?
Sharon: How would you guys like to have a taste test?
7-Year-Old: Like the Pepsi Challenge?
Sharon: Here it is. Everyone take a glass. (I admit, I watered down the juice a tad!)
7-Year-Old: It's watery.
6-Year-Old: Are we going to get some Pepsi?
5-Year-Old: It's OK.

Sharon: The juice is not really bad, is it? But, do you think it is as good as we were told it was?

Children: No.

Sharon: Why do you think we were told it was so good?

Children: Dunno.

Sharon: Do you think it was because they wanted us to buy it?

7-Year-Old: Yea. And you did buy it, too!

Sharon: Ah, yes, so I did. People make commercials to advertise a product. Sometimes the product is good and sometimes it isn't. When we see a commercial on television or on a billboard or we listen to it on a radio we have to judge if the product is really what it claims to be. Sometimes, advertisements are tricks. Sometimes we are tricked into buying something that is not very good or that we do not really want.

If the lesson ends right here, we already have introduced an important new idea: Advertising is meant to sell products. We also have introduced a key word to the children: Tricks! It was done in a totally non-threatening manner, using "taste" to drive home a message. Streetproofing often is the by-product of a well-rounded education.

Conversation continues:

Sharon: Sometimes people can play other kinds of tricks on people. Big people and little people can be fooled by tricks. Can you think of funny tricks people play?

7-Year-Old: You mean like the time Lester Bean covered all the girls' toilet seats in school with Saran Wrap, so they peed down their legs?

Sharon: Aah!

6-Year-Old: Like putting soap powder in the sugar bowl, or like the time our uncle filled the bathtub with green Jello or . . .

Sharon: OK. We know what we are talking about. Those tricks were meant to be funny and did no major harm, but I want to talk about other kinds of tricks now. For example: What if a big person, like a babysitter or older brother or sister, said to you, "All the candy bars in that store are free. All you have to do is take one without anyone seeing, put it in your pocket and leave the store." Now, do you think that is an OK thing to do?

5-Year-Old: Dunno.

7-Year-Old: That would be stealing, right?

Sharon: Yes, it would be. What would we have to say to the person who asked us to steal?

Children: No.

Sharon: Here is another example. What if a person bigger than you said, "Let's play a game. Every time I flip this penny and it lands on heads, you have to take off a piece of clothing. Do you think that is a trick?

7-Year-Old: That sounds dumb.

Sharon: If it sounds dumb, then what should you say to a person who asks you to do something like that?

Children: No.

Sharon: I don't think it is likely to happen to you, but if a big person ever moved into your personal space and made you feel uncomfortable or funny, you also should say No. Someone might try to touch your private parts, like your penis or vulva or chest, or maybe they won't touch you there at all but hug you when you don't want to be hugged, or tickle you when you don't want to be tickled.

If you ever find yourself in that position, I want you to say, No. Big people are not supposed to make little people feel uncomfortable. Big people *know* they are not supposed to do that.

If they touch you and make you feel bad inside, they may tell you not to tell anyone. They may say, "This is just a secret between you and me", or "If anyone found out about what we did, no one would love you and your parents would send you away." Now hold on, do you think your parents would send you away?

Children: No.

Sharon: Of course not. That would just be another trick!

All of the above took place in one session. If interest remains high, go over the material once more; if not, repeat it another time. Inundating children with too much information can cause problems.

Our hopes are that once children have been carefully, thoughtfully, and gently introduced to the ideas of tricks and secrets, they will be in a position to ask questions on their own. However, before they can do that, they must have an information base from which to ask their questions.

As a rule of thumb, try not to speak to your child about a particular topic for longer than five minutes at a time. Some might say this is four-and-a-half minutes too long. Judge for yourself.

Conversation continues:

7-Year-Old: Why?
Sharon: Why what?
7-Year-Old: Why would anyone want to touch me and make me feel uncomfortable?
Sharon: Sometimes big people have trouble making friends with people their own age, so they try to make friends with someone smaller. It is not wrong for a big person to be friends with a little person. But, if the big person plays a trick on you or makes you feel uncomfortable, I think you should tell someone. That's all.

Keep it simple. There is no need to go into elaborate descriptions of a pedophile.

Note: The five-year-old said little during our talk. She rolled around on the floor, staring longingly at the dark television set. The six-year-old seemed to be listening intermittently. A week later, her mother told me that during a television commercial the little girl had called out, "Look Mom, that man wants me to buy tires!"

What happens when an organization, such as Oxfam or UNICEF comes on the air to solicit funds for starving people? Our child may say, "Those people don't need money. It is a trick!" What can we say? We can tell them that not all commercials are tricks and continue the conversation:

"What do you think we can do to help these people?"
"We could send them food!"
"That is a very good idea. But it is hard to pack up food, and too expensive to mail a big package to a faraway place. What else could we do?"
"We could sent them some money. I have a dollar!"
"Let's do that. We'll put your dollar in an envelope and mail it to them. Maybe I could put in some money, too. I would never send money to someone I did not know. I know about

that organization. Please, do not give away your money to anyone unless you ask me about it. OK?''

This gentle approach also allows the child to feel she has some power, some control to change things in this world.

The Media

Why is it so important that young children are introduced to the powers of the media at a young age? How does the subject relate to streetproofing?

If we agree that self-esteem forms the foundation of well protected children, then the ability to discriminate is another working tool for their safety.

Our children receive powerful messages from the media. They are told that if you are rich, skinny, preferably white and have thick, luscious-looking hair, you will grow up to be popular and successful. We were never the age our children are now. Think about it — Rob and Laura Petrie of *The Dick Van Dyke Show* gave each other furtive pecks on the cheek before they turned out the lights. Their bodies never touched and Laura went to bed with more clothes on than we normally wear in a snow storm!

Our world is changing, our values are changing and television leads us down a merry path.

Examples:

''I put my three-and-a-half year-old son down for his afternoon nap in the family room. I looked in on him about half an hour later. There he was, glued to the television set, enthralled with a soap opera. A woman was giving birth and being incredibly vocal about it. That in itself was not bad. Thankfully, I discussed birth with him when I was eight months pregnant. But seeing the birth process in this manner, well, he became very frightened for me. He thought I might die.''

''Our four-year-old suddenly started to ask us if we were going to get a divorce. The question came right out of nowhere. 'Are you and Mommy going to live in different places one day? Who will I live with when you and Mommy don't like each other any more?' We were dumbfounded.

"It turned out that Mr. Rogers was spending the week talking about divorce. I have no qualms about that. I want my daughter to understand that some children live with one parent. She goes to a nursery school where many of her friends are from single parent homes. Now, we keep up. One of us tries to watch her shows with her, at least once a week."

There is no doubt that television can educate, by exposing our children to different cultures and ideas. It can encourage fantasy and make-believe. Yet, along the way, their eyes and ears may be damaged, their creativity stifled, their bodies left unexercised, and their senses may be dulled.

To say, "Turn the damn thing off," is not a practical idea. If you, like me, have reconciled yourself to live with television, here are some ways that might help tame the monster:

1. Sit down with your child once a week and, together, peruse the television guide section of your paper. Circle whatever is of interest to both of you. Set a time limit on TV watching, i.e. one hour during the day, one hour in the evening. Children have a marked preference for certain shows you may dislike. It probably would be a mistake to censor all the things they want to see. Balance. If your child wants to watch a "ride-em, shoot-em-up" show, so be it. Watch it with him.

2. As parents we tend to pick the shows we trust — Sesame Street, Mr. Dress-Up, Mr. Rogers, etc. Then we plant our children in front of the tube and leave. Do not leave. Once in a while, sit down with your child and watch these shows together.

3. Talk about the shows: "Do you think that blond lady is really so dumb?" "What would happen if we tried to drive our car on two wheels?" "Do you think a person could really jump through a window and not cut himself?" If your child shows interest in special effects, pick up a book on the subject. Demystifying the media is a good idea, as well as being educational.

Pornography

With the increased use of home videos our children are previewing movies once banned to them entirely.

Example:

"I am a working single parent. My seven-year-old daughter

gets home from school around 3:30 and rather than have her sit alone, I arranged with a neighbour to take care of her until 6:00. My neighbour's daughter who is ten years old goes to the same school, so my daughter is even escorted back to her home in the afternoon.

"One evening, I picked my daughter up and as we were walking home, she started talking about sex. I thought I was prepared to deal with this issue but she began to ask me about oral sex! My first thought was, Oh God, she has been molested!

"To make a long story short, it turned out that she and the other girl had been watching porno-flicks on the VCR. Where was my neighbour? Heaven only knows."

Pornography surrounds us and, at times, seems to engulf us. A walk down a city street now is a hazard. Poorly drawn posters of exotic dancers appear every few feet. The movie, *Not A Love Story*, produced by the National Film Board of Canada, states that there are four times as many pornographic bookstores in the United States than McDonald's Restaurants. What are we to say to our children? How do we begin to put into perspective this deluge of material intended to stimulate sexual desire?

We can start by examining our own actions and reactions. Let us say, we find ourselves in a convenience store with our six-, seven-, or eight-year-old child. Lo and behold, we spot a popular skin magazine. What are we to do? Do we shield her eyes and stampede out of the store? Do we comment loudly, making sure we have aroused the attention of all passers-by? Or can we seize the opportunity to talk to the child about our views on the subject. By all means, complain to the manager, by all means, let your opinions be known to your child, but not to the exclusion of her perceptions and points of view.

If you see the picture of a popular child nymphet on a billboard or in a magazine, ask your child how she feels about it. "How old do you think that girl is?" "Why do you think she is wearing makeup?" "Why do you think she is dressed that way?"

Evidence of sexuality is all around us. Let us use the constant intrusions of pornography to turn a negative experience into a positive lesson.

Censorship

Censorship is a mighty topic at the moment. The issue is not black or white and I, like most people, have stayed in the gray area. To suggest that the subject can be covered in a few paragraphs is to trivialize it. Nevertheless, if we are to bring up independent, free-thinking children it must, at the very least, be touched upon.

Censoring all books is not conducive to raising children's discerning powers. Censoring old classics which are considered racist will not allow them to understand the roots of racism, sexism, or bigotry in all their diverse manifestations.

Mark Twain's *Tom Sawyer* may serve as an example here, as could Shakespeare's *The Merchant of Venice.* If our ten-year-old is up to such in-depth reading, may we not simply ask her opinion? May we not point out that this is how black people were treated in Mark Twain's days. Ask, "Do you think people have come very far in their attitudes? If you were white, black, or purple, how would you feel about people treating you that way?" "Do you know what stereotype means?" "Do you think Jews, Blacks, Whites, etc. stereotype one another?"

Literature lends itself well to talking with children about subjects that normally do not come up in conversation. They can identify with the book characters and, with our help, stand back and judge the material and the author. By hiding from our children the bigotry of the past and present suggests that we should not tell them about the Irish Uprising, the Holocaust, the Christian Oppression, the incarceration of Japanese Canadians on Canadian soil during the Second World War.*

*If you are looking for excellent books on these topics, consult your local children's bookstore or ask the children's librarian at your library. On the topic of Japanese Canadians, I highly recommend *A Child in Prison Camp*, by Shizuya Takashima, Tundra Books, 1971.

We do not want to suggest that all bad things happened in the past; certainly, the nightly news can prove that point. The problem is not *what* is presented, but *how* it is shown. Allow your children to discuss their feelings, listen to their views and respect them, even if they don't quite match your own. Encourage them to "walk a mile in someone else's moccasins." You will promote empathy, decision-making, awareness, and knowledge. Isn't that what streetproofing is all about?

XVIII

STORYTIME

Where did our ability to weave a yarn go? Mention story-telling to a group of parents and watch them balk at the idea: "Who, me? I am not creative. I can't make up a story." Many of us believe that before we can begin a tale, we first must have a plot, then a theme, several characters, and, of course, an ending. Nonsense. All we need to tell small children a story is a beginning. When we then find ourselves at a loss for words, there is no need to panic; our children will continue and fill in the gaps.

Here is a familiar streetproofing story I recently told to a precocious six-year-old named Heather.

Susan Goes for a Ride

One day, Susan was playing on her front lawn. Uncle Bob pulled up in his neat new car. It was a convertible with a funny ornament on the hood. He asked Susan if she wanted to go for a drive. They even could go for an ice cream. Susan really liked Uncle Bob and wanted to go, but before she could get into his car or anyone's car, she had to do something first. What was Susan supposed to do? Right. She had to check first. She had to ask her Mom if it was alright. Susan's Mom might worry about her if she went off without telling anyone.

Susan got into the car. It smelled nice. Have you ever been in a brand-new car? What was the first thing Susan had to do when she got into the car? Right, she had to do up her seat belt.

It was a nice day. The sky was blue and the clouds were big and puffy. Looking up, Susan thought that one cloud looked like an elephant. She thought about what kind of ice cream she would have. Her favourite was pistachio but she liked peanut butter, too.

Then something funny happened. Uncle Bob put his hands between her legs. Isn't that a funny thing to do?

Heather thought this was a very funny thing to do. I then asked, "What do you think Susan should do?"

My little friend pondered and when I was about to continue the story without her response, she replied, "I don't know what she would do, but if I were her, I would put my hands between his legs to see how he likes it."

I have a problem. I believe children are never wrong and yet I thought this was as wrong an answer as I ever had heard. Then it dawned on me, no, she was right! That was the right answer. The wrong action perhaps, but the right answer, nonetheless. I asked, "Why would you put your hands between his legs?" She replied, "Because if he was going to make me feel bad, then I would want to do the same."

Had I responded to Heather's initial answer with what every fibre in my being wanted to say, "No, not that!," I also would have denied her the right to assert herself and protect herself in the way she perceived the situation.

If Heather were ever in a similar position, would she act in this manner? Hardly. She would be surprised, afraid, perhaps horrified. My concern was not to correct her response but to find a better one.

Having told the same story hundreds of times to many different children, I received a variety of answers. Boys typically respond by saying such things as, "If anyone ever did that to me, I'd beat him up." Girls, on the other hand, told me they would "jump out of the car." Occasionally, I heard the response, "Uncle Bob didn't know it, but in my back pocket I had a super X-ray gun that could blow him to smithereens!" A child who fantasizes to extract himself from a situation may not yet be prepared to handle the predicament. That's OK. If your child responds in a similar manner, forget streetproofing for today. Have some fun instead. The cavalry may come over the horizon, and Mightor may leap out of the clouds. A child's display of imagination is a far too precious thing to waste.

What *is* the right answer? Would we want Heather to say, "No, don't touch me. I want to go home." or "No, if you touch me like that, I will tell my parents." Let her phrase the words. We want the response to spring naturally from the child. Should Heather ever find herself in a similar predicament, we want her to KNOW the right answer, not search her memory for Mommy's reply.

If Heather believes herself to be in danger when the car

stops, she can get out and speak to the ice cream vendor. She can say, "Would you please call my Mom, I need help." However, if she has been told not to talk to strangers, is she likely to ask for help when she needs it?

Here are some other topics you may want to cover at storytime.

Jessica's New School

Jessica moved into a new house. Her Mom had been transferred from another city and she had to leave her old friends behind. She now would go to a new school. Jessica was very frightened about meeting all the new children. She wondered if anyone would like her. She put on her nicest clothes for her first day at school. Her Mom drove her to the door, and they both walked in to meet the principal. Soon, her Mom had to leave. It was awful. Jessica wanted to run to her and ask her to go with her. She was scared.

The principal took Jessica's hand and led her to her new classroom. Her teacher was a man and his name was Mr. Applebaum. Jessica had never had a male teacher before. He wore a yellow shirt and grey pants. He wasn't very old. He looked nice. Mr. Applebaum introduced Jessica to the class and showed her to her desk. Some kids started to giggle. Why do you think they giggled?

The recess bell rang and Jessica went outside with the rest of the children. She stood quietly by the door and watched the others play. No one seemed to care about her. Why do you think no one asked Jessica to play?

Finally, after a very long time, the bell rang and all the children went back inside. The morning passed and finally the noon bell went. Jessica did not go home for lunch because her Mom was working so she walked to the lunchroom. She sat down and began to eat. Jessica wished she had brought a book with her. She felt very conspicuous, alone.

Then three big girls sat down beside her. They started talking with her. Jessica felt funny but was glad she finally had someone to talk with. She wasn't sure about these girls; they were not in her class and things did not seem quite right. Have you ever felt that way?

One of the girls told Jessica that if she wanted to join their club, all she had to do was put a bottle of mouth-wash in the principal's desk. Jessica thought that was odd. She wanted to have friends, but didn't want to get into trouble. She said No. The girls called her a sissy. They said if she didn't do as they said, Jessica would be really sorry. She left the lunchroom and hurried back to her classroom. There was no one around and Jessica started to cry.

The afternoon passed and soon it was time to go home. She would have to let herself in because Mom didn't get home until five o'clock.

Waiting outside on the school steps were the three girls. They blocked Jessica's path. They called her a little coward. One girl actually shoved her.

How do you think Jessica felt? What could she have done? Go home?

At this point in the story, parent and child can talk about Jessica's problem. There is no perfect solution. Stories such as this one are meant to encourage empathy, in an attempt to understand the motives behind other people's behaviour.

Stories like this one are basic in plot but can be embellished with descriptions of people's clothes, their looks, and of the surroundings. Balance your story with big and little words, short and long sentences.

During storytime we can cover any topic under the sun. We even can introduce potentially scary situations. Watch the child's reactions. If he shows fear, manoeuvre the tale around, continue it, or end it quickly on a happy note.

Note: Do not use your child's name in the story. We want our children to sit back and analyze situations from a safe vantage point. Don't use the names of your child's best friends either. We don't want him to associate his best friend with the situation.

Stories for Children — Ages Three to Six

Here are a variety of short stories for young children. Read them aloud, add to them and change them around. Suddenly, you will find yourself making up your own.

Wednesday Nights

Jenny's parents always played tennis on Wednesday nights. The tennis courts were only one block away, so Jenny did not have a babysitter on those nights. She never felt scared because her parents were always home before dark.

One Wednesday night the telephone rang. Jenny said "hello" and the person at the other end of the line said, "Hello, who is this?" Now, that was a funny thing for that person to say. People who call us on the telephone are supposed to tell us who *they* are, not ask us to tell *them* who we are!

Jenny did not answer the question. All she said was, "What number do you want?" Do you think that was the right thing for her to say?

Saturday Picnic

Every summer, Tara and her family went to the beach for a big family picnic. It was always a wonderful day. Tara and her older brother Dennis would go beachcombing.

Once they walked a long way when they saw a man sitting on a beach towel. He waved, and Tara and Dennis smiled. The man got up and came over to them. He had a camera in his hand and asked them if he could take their picture. Tara and Dennis looked at one another. What was the harm? Dennis said he could take their picture but they first had to ask their parents. The man said it was silly to walk all the way back. Tara told him they were sorry but they had to speak to their parents first.

The man seemed angry but Tara and Dennis knew they were right. What would you do if someone asked to take your picture?

Cleaning Windows

Jeffery lived in a townhouse near a park. There were lots and lots of children around.

One day, he saw Mr. Roberts cleaning his windows. He was up on a ladder. He called Jeffery over and asked him to hand him the rag that had fallen down to the ground. Jeffery picked up the rag and gave it to Mr. Roberts.

The windows were soon clean and Mr. Roberts came down

the ladder. He then asked Jeffery to come into the house and have a lemonade. Jeffery said he would first have to ask his Mom. What would you do?

Maria

Maria's Mom had a new boyfriend named Philip. He was alright, maybe he was pretty nice, actually.

Mom said she was going to marry Philip. At first, Maria didn't like the idea, but then she decided that it was OK.

One night, Philip came to Maria's room to read her a bedtime story. He put his arm around Maria. It was nice. Then he started to touch her under the covers. That wasn't so nice. Maria told him to stop. She said it really loudly. Philip left the room.

Maria thought for a long time. She wondered if she should tell her Mom. Maybe her Mom would be mad but she decided to tell her, anyway. Would you tell if someone made you feel funny?

Rachel and David

Rachel liked to ride her bicycle up and down the street. She was a good bike rider. Sometimes, David would ride up and down the street with her. David was just learning. He was not as fast as Rachel.

One evening after dinner, Rachel and David were riding down the street. They decided to go into the park. The path was bumpy. Crash! David fell off. He hit his head. Rachel jumped off her bike to help David. He wasn't moving. His eyes were closed. Rachel was scared but then she took a deep breath and decided she needed help.

Rachel took off her sweater and covered David. She didn't move him at all. Then she remembered that he had his name written on paper in his pocket. She took it out and left it in plain sight.

Quick as light, Rachel hopped on her bike to go for help. She went to a small store at the corner and told the man behind the counter what had happened. He called an ambulance and the children's parents.

David was taken to hospital. He soon got better. It really

had been hard for Rachel not to panic. She had been scared but she knew she had done everything just right. What would you do if somebody had a bad fall?

Stories for Children — Ages Six to Ten

Alice's Story

"She scares me, Mom." Alice was seven years old and talking about old Mrs. Butterworth who lived on the first floor. "Alice Stuart," said her Mom in a very angry voice, "Mrs. Butterworth is a very nice, elderly lady. I want you always to be polite to her."

"But, Mom . . ." pleaded Alice. "No buts. I will not hear another word on the subject. If I ever catch you being rude to Mrs. Butterworth again, you will go to your room for a week. Do you understand me?" Alice understood alright. Mom could get pretty mad sometimes.

Alice wandered down the hall to her bedroom and looked out the window. A steady stream of cars was rushing along the highway. That was the best part about living on the seventeenth floor of an apartment building. She could see for miles and miles.

Dad would be home soon. It was a winter evening and the roads would be slippery, so he might be late. Alice would just have to wait before she could talk to him.

Finally, she heard Dad's keys jingle outside the apartment door. Before the key had turned in the lock, Alice ran down the hall and leaped into Dad's arms just as he was coming in.

"What's all this about?" laughed Dad. Alice buried her head in his shoulder and said in a muffled voice, "I want to talk to you about Mrs. Butterworth on the first floor."

"Oh, that," said Dad and put her back down. "Your mother called me at work and told me you had been rude to the old lady. She said that she was trying to be nice to you but you ran away. Is that true?" "Yes," said Alice meekly.

"Well, your Mother and I don't ever want to hear about you being rude to anyone, particularly to an older person who has no family, OK?" Dad kneeled down beside Alice and gave her a hug. "OK," said Alice quietly. "Good girl. Now, where is your mother?" Dad asked.

"On the telephone," said Alice, as she drifted down the hall to her bedroom feeling very sad.

Alice picked up her old ragged bear and began to cry. No one cares about me, she thought. No one cares how I feel. It's not that I don't like Mrs. Butterworth. I do. She is nice. She gives me candy and presents at Christmas. It's just that she keeps giving me big, sloppy kisses all the time and I don't like it when she pats my hair. She doesn't give Dad kisses and she doesn't pat Mom's hair. I wish we could move away. Finally, Alice fell asleep and didn't even wake up for dinner.

The next day, Alice went to school. Her teacher was called Miss Julie. She was the nicest teacher Alice had ever had. "Maybe," thought Alice, "just maybe Miss Julie could help me." At recess, she went up to her desk and stood beside it silently. Now that she was there, she couldn't think of a thing to say.

"What is it, Alice?" asked Miss Julie. "I . . . I want to move," stammered Alice. "Move? You want to change desks?" asked Miss Julie. "No, not my desk, my home." Oh, why were adults so dense? Why couldn't they just understand?

Miss Julie put down her pen, stacked some paper in a pile and moved them to the corner of her desk. "Alice, why don't you start at the beginning and tell me what is bothering you. Let's see if I can help."

Alice told Miss Julie about Mrs. Butterworth. She said that the old lady was really nice but kept hugging and kissing her.

At first, Miss Julie looked a little worried. She asked Alice some more questions. Then she turned to the blackboard and drew a picture of a lady. She said to the picture, "Mrs. Butterworth, I like you a lot, but please don't hug or kiss me anymore."

Alice thought that was funny. Imagine talking to a picture! She started to laugh and Miss Julie joined in.

"Now, Alice," said Miss Julie very seriously. "I want you to repeat that after me." "No, I can't. It wouldn't be very nice," said Alice.

"There will be lots of times in your life when you have to tell people how you feel. You and I both know that moving to a new apartment won't really solve the problem. I'm very glad you asked me to help. Your body belongs to you, Alice, and sometimes you just have to say it loud and clear. Do you understand?''

Alice said she did, even though she was a little confused. They both practised the little speech over and over and, after a while, Alice started to feel good about it.

Mom came to pick up Alice after school and the two walked home together. Just as they were entering the lobby, Mrs. Butterworth came toward them. She waved. Mom stopped to say hello.

"Well, Alice," beamed Mrs. Butterworth, "how was school today?" As she said that, she leaned down to give Alice a kiss. Her knees began to knock and her throat felt dry. Even her stomach felt funny. "School was fine, thank you, Mrs. Butterworth." replied Alice shyly. Would she say anything else? Would she ask Mrs. Buttewroth to please not kiss her anymore?

"Mrs. Butterworth, I like you a lot, but please don't hug or kiss me anymore." She had said it! Hooray!

Oh-oh! Mom sucked in her breath and stared at Alice. Mrs. Butterworth stood back, surprised. Now I'm in for it, thought Alice.

"You are perfectly right, Alice. I'm very sorry I made you feel uncomfortable. From now on, I'll just have to treat you like the grown-up young woman you are. From now on, we can shake hands or wave to each other. How about that?" Alice smiled. She really did like Mrs. Butterworth.

Note: A lot of attention is being placed on children protecting their private parts. That is not how non-violent sexual assault begins. Children should be made aware of anyone who intrudes on their private space. Was Alice in danger of being sexually assaulted? Probably not. However, in future, she will be better protected.

Questions:
1. What did you like about the story?
2. What didn't you like about the story?
3. What do you think would have happened to Alice had she not asked her teacher for help?
4. Do you think parents can sometimes be wrong?

5. What if Mrs. Butterworth had felt hurt because of what Alice said to her?

6. What if Alice's parents became angry with their daughter?

7. Was Alice right to tell Mrs. Butterworth how she felt?

You may wish to read the following story to your child, using it to answer some questions. On the other hand, you could read parts of it in an attempt to start a conversation. Then make up your own questions and responses and once again, form your own ending.

Barney's Story

Barney was eight years old. He had a sister named Barbara. She was ten. They lived with their Mom in a small town. Mom worked as a secretary in a steel mill. Their Dad didn't live with them anymore. He had moved to the city. Every second weekend Barney and Barbara got on a train to go and see their Dad.

Saturday rolled around and the children walked with Mom to the station. Barbara was all dressed up, as usual, and Barney was carrying a whole bunch of drawings. He knew Dad liked to see them. He would tape them to the fridge.

They kissed their Mom goodbye and got on the train. It was fun. They knew all the conductors by sight. Mr. Paul was their favourite. He always took good care of them. Once he even brought them up front to meet the train engineers and see the engine. Barbara decided right then and there that she was going to drive trains when she grew up.

Usually, they got seats together but today the train was packed. Barbara sat beside a lady who was reading a magazine. Barney sat beside a man who was asleep.

The train started and after a while the man woke up. "Well, hello," said the man in a surprised voice. "I must have dozed off." Barney and he began to talk, first about travelling, then about school, teachers and soccer. He showed Barney some pictures of his children and told him he was a soccer coach. Barney was impressed.

The train chugged along, stopping every half hour or so to

pick up and drop off passengers. It was a slow train. All of a sudden, the man got sick. He leaned forward, crossing his arms across his stomach.

"Oh," he groaned, "I'm afraid the motion of the train made me feel ill. I'd better go to the washroom."

Barney felt sorry for the man. It was never nice to see a person feeling ill. The man stood up and began to stagger down the aisle of the train.

"Can I help," asked Barney. "Thank you," said the man. Barney walked the man down the aisle of the train. They came to the washroom. The man stepped inside. "Won't you come in with me?" asked the man. "I may need your help."

Barney started to move forward but then moved back again. "It's OK. I'll wait for you here," replied Barney. "But, I need you," said the man.

"No." Barney didn't know why he had said no. After all, the man was nice, but . . . Just then, the man reached out and grabbed Barney. He was quick but Barney was quicker and he ran down the aisle in search of his sister.

"Barbara, Barbara . . .", he called out. "What's wrong with you?" she asked. "Barbara, the man, he . . ." sobbed Barney. "What are you talking about?" snapped Barbara. "Here, sit down," Barney slipped in beside her. He felt better. He was safe now.

"Tell me what's wrong with you," demanded Barbara. Brothers can be such a pain. "Nothing." Barney was snuggled in beside her for the rest of the trip.

Dad's apartment was really neat. It had been hard to understand why Dad had left home. Barney and Barbara had been really hurt and confused. That was a long time ago now. It was nice to be with Dad. They had gone shopping, had eaten in a restaurant and, to top it all off, they now were on their way to a movie. Barbara had a great time. Barney was very quiet.

After the movie, they went back to Dad's apartment. The two kids shared a room with yellow bunk beds. "Time for bed," Dad announced. Barbara went off but Barney sat down on the sofa. "I said bedtime, Barney." Dad had walked into the livingroom. "Yea, OK." Barney got up to leave.

"Hey, what's wrong with you, Sport?" asked Dad. "You've been dragging your tail all day."

"Nothing's wrong," said Barney, but he didn't move. He

wanted to tell Dad about the man on the train, but didn't know how. Maybe Dad would get mad at him. Anyway, what would he say? What did happen? All Barney knew was that he felt bad.

"Did you wake up feeling sad?" asked Dad.

"No."

"So, something happened today that made you feel down. Can you tell me when you started to feel this way?" Dad was good at asking questions.

"On the train," said Barney, very, very quietly.

"Tell me what happened on the train."

Slowly, he told Dad about the man on the train. Dad didn't take his eyes off Barney. He looked really upset. When Barney had finished, Dad got up and walked to the window. All of a sudden, he slammed his hand on the table. Barney jumped and started to cry. He knew this was all his fault. Dad was angry with him.

Finally, after what seemed to be a very long time, Dad turned to Barney and said, "I'm very angry, but I'm not angry with you. I think you did everything just right. I'm angry this thing happened to you. I think we should talk about it but I'm not sure how," Dad said scratching his head. "That man was wrong to make you feel uncomfortable, but you handled yourself really well."

"But, I was bad," said Barney.

"What are you talking about?" Dad was surprised.

"Mom told me not to talk to strangers and I did," said Barney.

"Do you think you could have sat beside someone for three hours without saying something?"

"I dunno," replied Barney.

"I know I couldn't. Barney, you did nothing wrong. You sat beside a man who seemed nice and when he got sick, you tried to help, right?"

"Yea."

"OK. Let's see what other things you could have done. If he really had been sick, do you think you could have helped him?"

"No," said Barney.

"Who could have helped?"

"Maybe Barbara. She's bigger than I."

"That's a good idea. What would Barbara do?"

"Um. She could have asked Mr. Paul, the conductor, to help the man." Barney was feeling much better now.

"What if Barbara was not with you?" asked Dad.

"I could ask for help myself!" Hurray for Barney!

"That's right!" Dad smiled. "Don't ever feel bad because you tried to help someone, Barney. But there is something I want you to remember. You come first. Your safety is important. That man was playing a trick on you. He pretended to feel sick, but wasn't. If he really would have been sick, he would have asked you to get help for him. How come you didn't go into the washroom with that guy?"

"I dunno. I just knew I shouldn't," said Barney.

"Your instincts told you not to go in there. You listened to your instincts and they kept you safe. I'm proud of you Barney. I really am."

They were quiet for awhile. Barney snuggled into his Dad's arms. "Why did he want me to go into the washroom with him?" wondered Barney.

"I guess he was a mixed-up guy who was looking for company. He might have wanted you to touch him or maybe he wanted to touch you."

"I don't get it."

Dad looked uncomfortable again. "He was mixed up. Maybe he wanted to make friends with people his own age but couldn't, so he tried to make friends with you."

"Do you mean that I can't every make friends with someone big?" asked Barney.

"You can make friends with someone big but if that person ever wants you to do something you don't want to do or tries to trick you or make you feel uncomfortable, that person is not your friend."

"He was a nice man, sorta," said Barney quietly.

"Maybe in some ways he was. But he was wrong to ask you to do something you didn't want to do. You were right to say no."

"What are we going to do tomorrow?" asked Barney.

Note: The word "sick" as related to the offender has been omitted in this story. Unless children have experiences to the contrary, most view sickness as something physical. Occasionally, in their need to categorize and understand the world around them, they will try to put the abuser's motives into their own perspective. They may ask, "Was he sick?" They may have heard from another source remarks about the abuser's behaviour, and the term "sick" used in reference to it.

If you choose to answer yes to the following question, do so with an explanation: "People who abuse children are sick, but it's a different kind of sickness than a tummy ache or the flu. We can't see it. It's a sickness some grown-up people have who do not understand right from wrong."

Buying Books for Children

There are many excellent books on the market dealing with the rites of passage children experience. Thousands upon thousands on a myriad of topics are aimed directly at children. Getting a divorce? Buy a book on divorce. A recent death in the family? Go out and get a book on the subject. A hospital visit coming up in the near future? Hurry. Buy a book. One has to wonder whether Mother Goose is at risk.

Books are a terrific resource for parents and children. They can open up a topic and further explain it. However, they do have their limitations. One cannot turn around the tale that already appears on the printed page.

Before you read a story to your child, read it yourself, first. Do you agree with the author? Is the book boring? Those with a message sometimes forget to entertain. Judge not only the content but also the illustrations. In one popular streetproofing book on stranger-danger, I noticed that the strangers were depicted as zoo animals. Most children become quite confused with books of this type. If a hippopotamus ever asked them to go somewhere with them, they surely would say no.

Examine the bindings. Will they hold up?

To what age level is the book directed? Don't be influenced by the notice on the cover that declares, "Recommended for Ages 3–5." Decide if it is appropriate for *your* child.

Look at the overall presentation. Can your child peruse it by herself after you have read it to her or is it a book that should be kept on the top shelf?

Books, videos, movies, plays are all aids we can utilize. However, nothing, absolutely nothing, replaces a caring parent who can talk openly to a child, face to face, about issues that concern them both.

A creative suggestion: It is quite likely that you will come across a book that is good in content but poor in production quality. The illustrations may be in black and white and your child loves colour. If the book is suitable for a child under five and does not have too many pages, photocopy it, colour in the pictures, and insert the pages in a spiral-bound photo album.

Testing Children

Children are good at learning by rote. Their abilities to memorize often are a source of amusement and pride for parents, grandparents and family friends. Children will supply the right answers to our questions but may have difficulty applying the knowledge to situations, particularly those that threaten their lives. How can we tell if a child has understood all you have said?

In Western society we have the answer we give tests. How do you know whether a child will or will not go with a stranger? Well, we could test her by leaving her in a park and asking a friend the child does not know to go there and see if he can lure her into his car. Think about it! What if the child *does not go* with the "stranger," but begins to panic? What if she *does go*? Are we then going to pop out from behind a bush and yell, "Ah, ha! Gotcha!" What would her reaction be to that? How would she feel? Humiliated, betrayed, confused, hurt. Are any of these feelings conducive to self-esteem? Such a test, therefore, could lead to unchecked fear and mistrust.

If you insist upon testing your child, do so in a manner that she will not perceive as physically threatening or emotionally damaging. For example, you might have a friend call your home while you are out. The Mom of your child's friend could invite him to dinner and say, "You don't have to call your Mom." See how your child responds. There are many other ways you could check to see if your message has been received.

XIX

INCEST

"The crimes of sexual intercourse or cohabitation between persons related within the degrees within which marriage is prohibited: sexual commerce of near kindred."
(*The Oxford English Dictionary,* Compact Edition)

Incest could be described as the most psychologically damaging abuse that can be inflicted, specifically, on a child. The above definition makes sexual intercourse contingent on incest when, in fact, from the victim's standpoint, penetration is not considered as the most destructive element.

For the purposes of this book, a better definition of incest might be, "The use for sexual gratification of a child (person) by another person who is considered by the child (person) to be a family member."

Small children do not understand bloodlines, intermarriage, etc. As such, anyone who a child perceives to be a relative and who, in turn, seduces the child is guilty of sexual abuse and incest.

Example:

If Uncle Seth, a close family friend, is introduced to Boy Rob as a bona fide uncle then Boy Bob will most likely come to love, trust and care for Uncle Seth in the same way most children care for their uncles. Should an abuse take place, Boy Bob will feel as betrayed by the family friend Uncle Seth as he would if he were indeed a true uncle!

In the case of extended family incest, the molester is more likely to be reported or, at the very least, the relationship will be terminated if the situation becomes known. Unfortunately, this is not always the case in "same premises" incests.

Most cases are either not discussed or kept quiet. Glynnis Walker, in her book, *Second Life, Second Best*, states that an estimated 75 to 90 per cent of child molestations within the family are not reported to any outside resource. What becomes of children when such practices are swept under the rug? How can they absolve themselves of shame and guilt? What are the guarantees that it won't happen again? Who will side with the child?

Example:

"He used to touch me, all over . . . No, he wasn't my father. He was, well, my stepfather. Oh God, I can't talk about this . . . What would it have mattered if he . . . we . . . had had intercourse? The damage was done.

"I'm married now, I have a daughter. No one knows . . . I'm only talking to you because there is a telephone between us. . . .

"You know what I get the greatest kick out of? Those coiffed women, you know the type, all talk and no experience. . . . They say things like, 'Don't let anyone touch your private parts.' Do they think I let him touch me? Do they think he asked my permission?''

The reverberations of molestation by a relative affect children's abilities to trust, to believe in people. It shakes them to the roots and may destroy their very lives. The experience leaves deep and damaging scars. Few recover; those who do harbour resentment and mourn their lost childhood. Pure and blinding hatred may be extended, not only to the abuser but to all those who surround the abuse.

Example:

"My mother should have known. She says she didn't. She brought this guy, my supposed stepfather, into the house. She looks me in the eye now and says she didn't know. Where did she think he went for hours on end?

"We lived in a small house. If he wasn't in the kitchen and not in the livingroom and his boots and hat were on the hook, where did she think he was? Why didn't she look for him? Why didn't she check on me at night?

"I think I hate her as much as I hated him. All she cared

about was her meal ticket; it didn't matter to her who paid for it."

Stepfathers, according to researchers, are five times more likely to sexually abuse their stepchildren than natural fathers. It is estimated that over one million American women have been molested by their fathers or stepfathers. Does this suggest that our boys are risk-free? Incidents of male child incestuous molestation are not as high, but we cannot assume that boys are excluded from them.

"Parents who remarry must forearm their children by providing appropriate knowledge on molestation." Over the years, I have made that statement to many classes of parents. The responses I received often astonished me:

"My children did not want me to remarry after their father died. They were very upset when I did marry. If I had told them about this molestation stuff, they might have used it to get rid of my present husband."

"Don't you think that talking about this sort of thing to children might jinx a new marriage?"

"What if my fiancé heard me telling my children about sexual molestation and incest. He might think I don't trust him."

"If I ever had given the matter a moment's thought, I would never have remarried."

At the risk of further repeating myself, let me say again that our own sensitivities and situations must *never* come before our children's safety.

The following is the case study of Wendy, the eldest child in a family of eight children. Four of the five girls were repeatedly sexually molested by their natural father.

Wendy's Story

Where should I begin? Maybe I'll start with the present. I'm divorced now and have two boys. I work in a bar. I'm the best bartender you'll ever meet. I don't drink or smoke, have never touched drugs, and I definitely don't sleep around. My neighbours think I'm an enigma.

I was eight or so when he (father) started on me. There is a lot I don't remember. He never actually penetrated me. He saved that for the next sister. . . . No, I never knew . . . that he was also abusing her. I didn't know until years later.

Around sixteen or so, I was kicked out. I started to rebel, you see. Oh, he hadn't bothered with me for a few years, at that point. I don't know when it stopped. I was kicked out of the house on some lame-brained excuse. My greatest fear had come true — expulsion.

That is what he used to threaten me with. I was terrified of being sent away. Whenever I misbehaved, he said I would be sent to a convent. Can you imagine what that meant to me? The only security I had ever known would be taken away, unless I danced to his tune. If I didn't behave, I was out. One day, I was out.

No, I never told anyone. Who was there to tell? Well, once I did mention to the school guidance counsellor that I was unhappy at home. She called up my folks and told them. She betrayed me. I never spoke with her or anyone else again. I have a theory, you tell another person a secret and they have control over you. They have power over you. I know all about power and control.

After I left, the family really went to hell in a handbasket. Up until then, we hadn't moved around much, but after I was gone, they didn't stay in one place longer than six months or so. A neighbour once said, quite innocently, of course, that I was the glue that held the family together.

I never had friends or boyfriends for more than a few months. I wasn't a pretty child, at all.

Where was my mother during all of this? Making babies, I guess. There is a lot I have forgotten, but some instances are as clear as a window. The night my sister Charlotte was born, the hospital phoned. I was in bed with him when he picked up the receiver.

My mother and I have never talked about him and what he did. She never spoke to me after charges had been laid. I remember her once accusing me of coming between her and my father. I was eleven at the time.

Charges were laid after I found out that he was abusing my sisters. You see, there is a five-year span between all the girls, all but one girl, Lorie. I don't think he ever touched her. Besides, Lorie was a blabbermouth. She was only a year younger than Jennifer. He raped Jennifer.

The charges were laid. Children's Aid was involved but we had this really young worker. He didn't know what he was doing. We were his first incest case. Charlotte met with him a few years back. He apologized to her. Needless to say, our father got off.

I often wondered why he (father) did it. As far as I knew, he was never molested as a child. My aunt, his sister, is a social worker (she is on our side), and she doesn't know of any incident in his past that would have led him to do what he did.

Once, I was five I think, I was walking home from some place and an old man on a bicycle stopped and offered me a ride in exchange for a kiss. A ride was a ride, right? My parents found out and got really upset. Sometimes, I wonder if maybe that incident set everything off. Did he figure I was tainted somehow? Did that (incident) give an edge to his reasoning?

It's not over. I swear he will not get away with it. I'm tired of hearing excuses for molesters. My brother takes his three-year-old daughter to visit them for the weekend. Can you believe that! He is divorced from his wife. She got a court order barring him from taking the child up there and he (my brother) got a court order against her court order. You know what my brother says? "Oh, he's an old man now. He's past all that stuff." Was he going through a phase, and now it's all over?

This abuse, it didn't affect me badly, it affected me profoundly! My other sisters are all doing well, coping. One would probably assume that because of our childhood we would end up on the street. Actually, the opposite happened. All of my sisters went on to university. One of them will soon have a Ph.D.. Another is happily married, one is in an executive position, and I plan to return to university soon.

I sometimes think that other people assume incest victims wear a brand on their foreheads or have horns on their heads. It irks people somehow to find out that their best friends, their neighbours, have been molested.

Get even, yes, I'll get even. I can't murder him, I have two boys to think of. He wrecked a lot of lives and I won't let him wreck my kids'. Besides, murder is too easy. I think about how I'll get even.

What's he doing now? He's a high school teacher. . . .

One thing is clear, secrets are a must when it comes to incestuous molestations. Wendy and the other sisters who were involved, kept a code of silence. Wendy told the guidance counsellor just once that she was unhappy at home. The counsellor, in good conscience, relayed the information to her parents without finding out why she was unhappy. Feeling her confidence betrayed, Wendy retreated into a world of silence and the molesting continued, from one child to the next.

XX

CHILD STEALING NON-CUSTODIAL ABDUCTION

Why would a parent steal his or her own child? Out of love? Taking the child away from all that is familiar — home, grandparents, school, clubs, sports, the other parent — is that love? Parents, usually non-custodial parents or those in the midst of a separation, steal a child for revenge. And does it work!

We can imagine what happens to a parent whose child has been abducted. After the initial shock the search begins. Months, even years may pass. The trail grows cold. The police file away the case in the hope that new evidence may, one day, be uncovered. Meanwhile, finances have dwindled and the searching parent begins to flounder.

"Children who were taken by one of their parents are in safe hands. After all, they are with a parent," is the opinion of many, if not most individuals.

Teachers, principals, and those who work with children, are in the best position to spot abducted children because many abductors enroll them in a school, somewhere. They usually do to prevent drawing attention to themselves. That is why all schools should demand a child's previous school files. Although this is required by law, many schools do accept a child and wait for the files to follow. In abduction cases, the school will have a long wait.

Are children safe while in the care of the parent who abducted them? Sally Abhrams, author of *Children in the Crossfire*, states: ". . . The psychological and physical scars inflicted by 'loving' abductors are commonplace, rather than rare. Sexual or physical abuse is standard fallout from the war between the parents. Child Find, Inc., a New York support group for victims of child stealing, maintains that the majority of snatched youngsters are beaten, sexually molested, or neglected with fathers more likely to be violent and mothers neglectful. The group contends that these parents do love their children but love under pressure creates violence. Another organization in California surveyed five hundred snatchers and found 90 per cent had a history of physical or emotional abuse.''

Picture this scenario: A child is kidnapped from school. She is thrown into the back of a car, seemingly without rhyme or reason. Under the cover of night, she is motored to an unknown destination. Perhaps, she is told that she is on her way to a better life, but she might be told nothing and is too frightened to speak. Life on the road is hard. Where can the parent get a job? A social insurance number is now all but useless as are other identifications and/or credit cards. The homes of friends and relatives are out-of-bounds as the abductor is or will be under surveillance. Children on the road are often forced to change their names and their appearance. They live a lie and know it.

Without friends or family, how long will it be before the child is abused? How long before the abducting parent takes out his/her frustration on the child? A parent who kidnaps is in a perpetual state of fear. He is angry and the anger that once was directed at his spouse now is focused on the child.

Would the abductor talk kindly about the absent parent? Hardly. The child is told that their missing Mom or Dad is a drunkard or dead. The physical barrier set up to prevent the child from escaping, eventually becomes a psychological one.

Sally Abhrams: ''Cruel but clever abductors often use sophisticated psychology to beguile their trusting children. 'One time, my brother and I had a fight,' recalls a still baffled youngster. 'My father said, 'You're such a bother, I may as well send you back to your Mother.' 'I was so confused. I was dying to go back to my Mom, yet he was saying your punishment for acting up is going home. I started to think if that was what I got for being bad, Mom mustn't be so great.'

''The left-behind parent is transformed into the bad guy by an architect who masterminds a perverted plan. Snatchers may tell home-sick children that their missing mother or father knows where they are and is not interested in retrieving them, or that their parent has a new husband or wife and children and no longer needs them. Not showing up is proof that the parent does not love the child. The rejection can be unbearable. One child was despondent because she was convinced her mother wasn't interested in fetching her. 'I asked Dad if he was going to call Mom and tell her where we were and he said he already had, so I thought she knew.' "

Examples:

"My ex-boyfriend, the father of my two lads, says he's gonna take them and I'll never see them again. He's got a gun. Once he got drunk and said he was goin' ta kill me. He shot up the house instead."

"My ex-son-in-law was in jail on a fraud charge. We were told he would not get out for three months but he turned up on my wife's doorstep thirty days later while I was at work. He wanted to know where my daughter and granddaughter were living. My wife refused to tell him. He beat her up. Finally, my wife told him where they were, I think he would have killed her if she hadn't. As he was leaving, he stole a bottle of liquor. Luckily, he took the time to drink it. My wife phoned our daughter and she and our four-year-old granddaughter made a run for it."

"Before all this mess began, we lived the good life, or so I was told. My marriage collapsed and my husband kidnapped the two boys. I sold the house and spent every cent of the money looking for them. My parents took out a mortgage on their home and hired detective after detective. My mother had a stroke and my father has since died of a heart attack. I spent years looking for them. Finally, I remarried and had another child. Forget them? Not for one second. My sons became ghosts in my new marriage. After eight years, I received a telephone call. My ex-husband said he would return them if I dropped all the charges. Both boys had been badly abused, physically and psychologically. There was no joyous reunion. We are coping. One son is in trouble all the time, both are in therapy."

What can we do?

If marital problems are on the horizon or there are threats of abduction, consider the following preventative measures:

- Obtain one passport made out in your child's name. Inform the passport office that if a second application is made, you want to hear about it. Two legal passports cannot be issued under the same name.
- Keep up-to-date pictures of your children.
- If a break-up is imminent, immediately obtain a temporary custody order. Have several certified copies made and give one to your child's school, along with a picture of your estranged spouse. Most parental kidnappings take place during the time of marriage break-up and divorce.
- Make sure the custody order details police procedure. If the order is violated, the court will give the police specific authorization to retrieve the child.
- The custody order may include a clause restricting access to school records. If such is the case, inform the school yourself of this order.
- Keep a running list of all pertinent information concerning your estranged spouse — license numbers, credit card numbers, etc. Maintain a list of all addresses and phone numbers of his/her relatives and friends.
- The ex-spouse or individual who has made overtures to abduct can be ordered by the court to post a sizeable bond. If the child is taken, the money can be used to aid in the search.
- Stay in contact with your ex-in-laws. If the divorce has been particularly messy and the in-laws have sided with their offspring, try writing to them once a month, using as an excuse their interest in the child's accomplishments.
- Work out amicable visiting rights. Parents who are satisfied with the arrangements are less likely to abscond with a child.
- Teach your children their area code and phone number. Make sure they always have some quarters on them. (While it is not necessary to tell them to hide the money, you must say, "Don't tell anyone about the quarters you have on you. It is no one's business but your own.")
- Give your children passwords. Tell them they are not

allowed to go with anyone — not even Daddy/Mommy — unless the password is used.

- See that your child uses the "buddy system." Encourage him/her to walk to and from school with a friend.
- State clearly to your child that if all his/her friends are leaving the park, you want him/her to come home too.
- Implement a Safe Arrival Program at your school.
- Always tell your children you love them. Tell and show, tell and show. . . .

Note: Non-custodial kidnapping is an escalating crime, one that cuts across all class barriers. It deserves in-depth study.

XXI

LATCHKEY KIDS

By definition, latchkey kids are children who are on their own for more than one hour per day. While most children under ten years of age will have some sort of supervision throughout the day, increasingly, small children are left to their own devices for a variety of reasons.

We assume that latchkey kids are from single-parent households or from homes where both parents work outside the home. As a result, many children must fend for themselves before and after school and even those who are supervised full time often are left on their own for brief periods; for example, Mom may pop out to the store or either parent may be in the shower. The child may rise at six in the morning and meander around the house for two hours; Mom may take Susie to the dentist while Johnny remains behind.

While we do not want to encourage independence to the point of abdicating our own role as protectors, we do want to develop in our children the kind of self-reliance or self-sufficiency that will protect them, should an occasion arise when they must be left on their own.

We can prepare for the unexpected, at least to some degree, by consciously allowing our children privileges for behaving in an acceptable manner.

Privileges and/or Rewards for Very Young Children:

Behaviour	Reward
Played nicely for a whole hour with other children.	A big hug and an extra bedtime story.
Did not open birthday girl's presents at her party.	A special treat on the way home.
Did not sit on the dog or pull his ears for a whole week.	A trip to the zoo.

Older children will benefit from seeing a posted list of privileges. They do not have to be able to read.

Behaviour	Reward
Coming home directly after school to change into playclothes.	Stay up an extra hour on Friday night.
Sitting through a restaurant meal without flicking peas at the waiter.	Extra spending money.
Turning off the TV after favourite show without being told to do so.	A Saturday morning without chores.
Playing with baby sister for a whole hour.	Choice of menu on Saturday night.

When we think of consequential behaviour, we tend to view it in the negative, i.e., "If you pull the dog's tail, you will get bitten and find yourself in your room for an hour." By writing out consequences for appropriate behaviour we are showing children that good deeds will be rewarded.

Coping with Fear

Children who find themselves on their own for whatever reason, must learn to come to terms with numerous problems. Fear is one emotion often experienced by the latchkey child. While we cannot eliminate it, we can help the child cope with it.

To enter an empty house or apartment all by yourself can be scary. Houses make different sounds when no one is around. Many children are not allowed to leave the house after school. They are told to come home, lock the door, not answer the door, and not have friends over. While these rules might minimize physical danger, they tend to enhance or give validity to fear. Above all else, we want our child to feel secure. This elusive security helps to combat fear and, in turn, helps a child to cope.

Examples:

"My two-year-old son was convinced there were monsters in his room. I tacked a sign on the door that read, 'No Monsters Allowed.' It worked!"

"I remember that all the closet doors in my room had to be shut tight every night. That didn't help. I was still very sure that a bear was in my closet. One night, my Dad came into my room with a big stick. He went into my closet, closed the door behind him and proceeded to beat my clothes. He came out all dishevelled, huffing and puffing. He said he had killed the bear. I thought that was really funny and that was the end of my fear."

Here are some creative suggestions that can be applied not just to latchkey kids but to all children:

1. Sit down with your child and together listen to all the house sounds — the fridge, branches tapping at the window, dogs barking, cats mewing, the gerbil running in his cage. Can you hear the apartment building's elevator? How does it sound when neighbours pull up in the driveway or open the door across the hall?

2. Walk over every square inch of your house or apartment together. Slam doors, close and open windows, check locks, turn lights on and off, (check for burned-out light bulbs), rattle doorknobs, look under beds and in closets. Do this exercise during the day and at night. The world is different after nightfall. Ask your child to tell you what seems spooky to him. Is he afraid of a hand coming from under the bed that will grab him? Does he think a bad man will get him as he runs up the basement steps? Do not dismiss these fears. Talk about them.

3. Walk around the outside of your house together. Ask your child, "What if you came home and saw the front door lying open. What should you do?" Tell her that if she ever saw such tell-tale signs of a break-in, she is not to enter the house but go directly to a neighbour or the home of a Block Parent.

4. Get to know your apartment building intimately. How many exits are there from and into the garage? Follow the stairs up and down. Is it possible for an inquisitive child to get up onto the roof unobserved?

5. If you have glass doors, install locks that can be opened with a key from the outside as well as the inside. One of the easiest ways to gain entry to a home is to break a window and then open the door from the inside. Better yet, have a security inspection done on your home.

6. If your child is to return home after dark, especially in the winter, put several lights including the outside porchlight and perhaps a radio on a timer.

7. If you own a coffee maker with a timer, consider buying hot chocolate packages that mix with water. Set the timer to coincide with your child's homecoming. While this might not be a nutritious suggestion, a child will welcome a hot cup of cocoa on a cold winter evening. Apply caution to prevent burns.

8. Leave a welcome-home note.

9. Lost keys are big problems for little kids. Discuss contingency plans. Is it possible to leave a key at the neighbour's home? Avoid leaving extra keys under the flowerpot, the door mat or above the door frame.

10. Tell your child what to do in case of:
   — a thunderstorm: Unplug the television set and remove the rabbit ears; do not go outside, etc. It also is a good idea to talk about being caught outside in a thunderstorm.
   — a fire: Get out of the house and call the fire station from a neighbour's home; sound the alarm in the apartment and get out!

11. Make a familiar noise when you (parent) enter the house. Jingle your keys outside the door or have a special knock. Never, ever sneak into the house when your child is alone.

12. Make sure your child knows where you are. (See Home Communications Centre, Chapter VII)

Making Your Home Safe

Eliminate as many potential hazards as possible — take up loose rugs from the floor, make sure tapwater is not too hot, keep stairways clear of paraphernalia.

Equip your home with a first-aid kit. While many families claim to have such a kit in their homes, it often is in an awkward place or not well stocked. Aspirins need not be part of the kit, however, Band-Aids, iodine or a similar preparation, as well as ointments for minor burns, are essential.

Keep a safety box in your home. Make sure it is easily accessible, even when the lights are out. The box should contain: a flashlight, candles and waterproof matches (for older children); extra fuses, a pen, paper, tape, scissors. Naturally, a fire extinguisher should be near by. Does your child know how to operate it?

Naturally, you have fire detectors in your home. Many detectors have been known to go off on their own if poorly situated, or they may sound the alarm because of a piece of burnt toast. In such cases, what is your contingency plan?

Children must know how all the locks work and, if applicable, how to turn on and off alarm systems.

Get rid of the old unused fridge in the basement. Talk about how to have a safe playtime when you are away.

If you live in an apartment building with an elevator, talk to your child about being stuck in it. Do so while the two of you are inside the elevator.

Note: On certain models, the emergency buttons are at the top of the panel. When I questioned the superintendent of a large apartment complex about this I was told, "We chose this elevator because kids kept fooling around with the emergency buttons. Now, they can't reach them."

Most parents will not allow their children to use the stove when they are alone. If that is the rule in your home, leave a snack for your child.

You likely will have discussed answering the phone with your children. As they look upon the telephone as their survival line, tell them how to deal with a broken line.

Keep pen and paper beside the phone for messages.

Few children benefit from being on their own at a young age. Before you consider leaving yours to their own devices for several hours, every day, check out the resources in your area. The local library may run an after-school program; call up your local YMCA or similar association and investigate. Do not rule out day care centres. Having seen the great need for after-school programs, many of these centres accept older children for specially designed programs. Some cities now have hotlines for latchkey children. If your area has one, post the number by the telephone.

Children who cannot cope with being left alone will find a way to tell you so. Their message may be subtle or very overt.

Example:

"I left for work at 7:30 every morning. My seven- and eight-year-old boys left for school at 8:15. Every day, I would set a timer to ring at precisely 8:10, and would phone at 8:20 just to make sure they had made it out the door.

"I was always worried about them, and would arrive home before they did. One afternoon, I found my house all but destroyed. Plants had been tipped upside down, chairs and tables were turned over, drapes had all been pulled down. What a mess! I was about to call the police when I realized that nothing had been broken, nothing was missing, and the doors and windows had not been tampered with. My youngest son was definitely telling me something.

"We talked about it. I had assumed he had done this in a rage, but no, he said he had gone methodically around the house carefully tipping things over. He said he didn't want to break anything!"

XXII

BABYSITTERS

Few of us can forget the first time we hired a babysitter. Regardless of how much confidence we had in our chosen caretaker, it was a nerve-wracking experience.

When our children are very young, we tend to be very thorough in our search for the perfect sitter. We ask questions and check references. As infants become toddlers and toddlers reach first adolescence, we become more confident, and sometimes let down our guards. A mother of a parenting organization once stated, ". . . As children grow older, parents do not really see the child as quite so helpless and tend not to take the same precautions. . . ."

Do not let up. Scrutinize each applicant, regardless of the ages of your children. Babysitters must be able to represent us in our absence. While we may try to limit their authority, children do look upon them as our temporary replacements.

How to Find One

1. Ask your friends but do not be surprised if many parents are reluctant to give away the names of their best babysitters. Ask anyway.

2. Phone the nearest day care centre, nursery, or playschool. Many day care workers babysit during the evening. They also may have the names of other people who do.

3. If your local community college has an early childhood development course, give them a call. College students may demand more money but have a vested interest in being with children. Some colleges even give students credit for babysitting. This too can work to your advantage. Do not assume that all college students have nine-to-five hours; many have the odd free day and might welcome a part-time job.

4. Call up the Red Cross or St. John's Ambulance to enquire whether they offer babysitting classes. If they do, ask the

course instructor to recommend the best students. Be prepared to answer personal questions.

5. Churches and organizations such as Girl Guides also might give you a hand in your search.

Hiring

1. Your first contact with an applicant probably will be over the phone. State your expectations, not in detail at this point, but if you at least mention your basic requirements and needs you will save everyone's time and energy. Ask how much the babysitter expects to be paid. Make arrangements to meet and ask the applicant to bring along a list of references.

2. Many people feel applicants should come to interviews alone. I strongly disagree. If your prospective babysitter is a teenager who is unknown to you, ask that a parent or guardian accompany her. You also may be skeptical of any parent who allows her/his teenager to go alone into an apartment building or house. If the parent is unwilling or unable to come, suggest the applicant bring a friend. Should she do so without your prior invitation, do not discredit her. Put yourself in her shoes. Would you go into an unknown house alone?

3. Talk openly to your future babysitter. While you do have to discuss household rules, and while it is true that a babysitter is an employee, it is to your advantage to establish a warm working relationship with that person.

4. Pose a few hypothetical questions: "What would you do if Billy swallowed something and started to choke?" "What would you do if someone came to the door and said he was my son's uncle and wanted to take Billy for a walk? What if he showed you his ID and proved he was, indeed, Billy's uncle?" If the second question has been answered, you may well ask why she would open the door in the first place.

5. Ask your would-be babysitter why she wants to babysit. Most self-respecting teenagers will openly admit that they want extra pocket money. If that is the only reason, then you might not want to employ her. However, do not expect to be given purely altruistic reasons. A welcome answer would be, "I'm good with kids, and I need the pocket money", or "I'd rather be with children than pack bags at the food store." Another

honest response might be, "Next year I am going into early child development in college. I'd like some experience with children."

6. Ask your would-be babysitter about her own interests. Do they all centre around children and child care? Does she have friends her own age? Is she involved in activities suited to her age group?

7. Call each reference on the list. Ask specific questions such as, "How long has Martha been working for you?" "How old are your children?" "Has she ever cancelled out on you? Was it for a valid reason?" "Do your children ask for her to babysit?" "Has she ever handled a crisis in your household?" "Have you ever had any problems?" "How did you come to hire Martha? Is she the daughter of your best friend?" "What duties does she do in your home? Does she bathe your children?" Write out your questions beforehand. (As a general rule, I do not recommend babysitters be allowed to do the bathing, unless the child has had an accident, such as spilling a bowl of soup. This is particularly important when the sitter is taking care of more than one child. If the one is in the bath, it stands to reason that the other one will be left unsupervised. If possible, whenever you hire a babysitter for the evening, feed and bathe the children yourself before you go out, or ask the babysitter to come early. Pay her a little extra to do both jobs while you still are present.

8. Before leaving your babysitter in charge for the first time, have her visit the children while you are there. Let them get to know her.

9. Arrange pick-up and delivery of your babysitter well ahead of time. As the employer of a young person, you must accept the responsibility of her safe conduct home.

10. It would not be out of line to ask your babysitter to take a first-aid course. There are many such classes available. Check out your local Red Cross, St. John's Ambulance, or community college. These courses usually are inexpensive and you might arrange to pay for the course in exchange for a certain number of free babysitting hours. If hiring is contingent upon successful completion of such a course, the employer should pay for it outright.

11. Be open and honest about problems that exist in your family. This does not mean an accounting of all your personal

business, but if you are a single parent with ex-spouse difficulties, say so. If warranted, give your babysitter specific instructions on how to handle your ex-spouse, should he/she appear at the door or telephone. If non-custodial abduction is a worry to you, then extra directives will be necessary. On no account is she allowed to hand over the children to your ex-spouse. Show your babysitter where you keep the certified copy of your separation agreement. If necessary, give her permission to call the police.

12. Talk over with your babysitter all household rules while the children are present. Be specific without playing the authoritarian. The rules should be short and to the point, designed to apply to babysitter and children alike.

Example:

"Honestly, I went to babysit at this house and the mother handed me a fourteen-page, hand-written list of rules and regulations. She left with her husband right away, and I was supposed to take care of three kids and read that stuff at the same time!"

13. Do not hold back necessary medical information concerning your child. If she has asthma or is prone to epileptic seizures, say so. Give your babysitter some pamphlets on the topic, however, do not expect her to delve into six-inch-thick medical textbooks.

14. Discipline always is a touchy subject when dealing with a babysitter. Religion and politics are tame stuff compared to child-rearing because most of us have very definite ideas on it. Therefore, do not assume your babysitter will adhere to your standards just because you have stated them. Be nosey, come back two hours ahead of time, listen at the door. If this sounds unduly paranoid, so be it. I am talking about our children here.

15. Show your babysitter the Household Constitution or Bill of Rights (see Chapter VII). Explain what each right means. Specifically, mention that yours is a streetproofed household State, "In this home we do not keep secrets."

16. Point out all possible fire exits. Talk about fire. Show your babysitter how the locks work and, if applicable, how to shut off alarms that go off accidentally.

Note: Someone other than yourself should have the phone number of your babysitter, especially Dad at work.

No doubt, you noticed my constant reference to babysitters of the female gender. It is unfortunate that we normally do not hire boys for the job. Males often are viewed as "too experimental," the connotation being, "they may try something." It is important for our children to see boys in protective and caring roles. This is not to suggest that we should immediately march out and find ourselves a bevy of male babysitters. However, if a boy does apply for the job, do not disqualify him outright; scrutinize his abilities, experience, and background in the same way as you would a female babysitter.

What to Expect

1. Babysitters should cancel only in cases of emergency or illness. Many phone at the last minute leaving parents in the lurch for other reasons, usually a hot date. When that happens, find a new sitter.

2. Unless you have a "calls waiting" system on your telephone, babysitters should not use the phone to chat with friends for hours on end. There is nothing more disconcerting than trying to reach someone at home, only to find the line busy.

3. Friends should not be allowed over, unless you have given permission in advance, and then only those you know personally. Friends of the opposite sex should never be allowed to come over. Period. You are hiring a person to do a job. Would she expect to bring friends to her office? Hardly.

4. No Smoking!

5. You may want to tell your babysitter that your young child is not allowed to eat certain foods, such as popcorn, grapes, hot dogs, peanut butter, etc. All of these foods have been known to choke children.

7. Do not forget to leave some food for your babysitter. Point out what she may eat. If you do not, don't be surprised if your smoked salmon has disappeared.

8. Pay your babysitter on time. This seems an obvious statement, however some parents find themselves short of cash or without change. Promising to pay the next time is not a good

policy. If it is your habit not to carry cash, and you use a particular babysitter often, work out a payday schedule and stick to it.

Note: If for some reason, you cannot get home, do you have the phone number of the superintendent of your apartment building with you, or that of a neighbour who can make a quick check for you?

Preparing Your Child

Most children have had ample experience with babysitters since before they were two years old. As each new person is introduced to the household, it will be to everyone's benefit if your child has been prepared in advance. Here are a few ideas to which you can always add new ones:

- Play peek-a-boo with your child.
- Let him play alone in a room for brief periods.
- Talk about the babysitter in advance. Describe her to your child.
- Leave a special treat or snack or buy a small gift for your child to be opened after you leave the house.
- Tonight might be the night when you allow your child to stay up for an extra half hour.
- If you own a VCR, pick a special movie everyone can watch. Do not provide popcorn. If you do not own a VCR, and as a very special treat you could rent a movie projector from your local library.
- Do not tell your child to be good and do what the babysitter says. Abolish such words from your vocabulary; they don't mean anything. They also contradict everything you have said before about trusting one's instincts.

Small children show definite preferences of who they like and who they don't like. Pay attention to the signals. Most children cry when Mom and Dad leave; if the crying persists for a long time, something is not quite right. You can get an idea how your child feels about her new babysitter by playing the following game:

The Hat Game

Children love to wear hats. Keep some old ones in the playroom. To play the Hat Game put a hat on your head and another one on your toddler. Tell her you are the babysitter and then act out her role as you perceive it. Now exchange hats and say, "You are the babysitter now, and I am the baby." Play for awhile and then do something out of the ordinary such as throwing a doll across the room and stamping your feet; say No loudly. Watch the child's reaction.

Example:

"I hired an older woman to babysit my three-year-old son. She came well recommended although one mother told me she ran a tight ship. I hired her fulltime and for awhile everything seemed to be fine. She cared for my son and often did little things around the house. Yet I felt uneasy. To this day I don't know why. Then little things started to happen. My son began to wet his pants and became very clingy. At first I didn't pay that much attention to it.

"Finally, I tried playing the Hat Game with him. I let him be the babysitter. He didn't do much at first. I then decided to act up a bit. I put a toy under my foot and stepped on it. By accident, I actually broke it. My son looked at what I had done and burst into tears. Initially, I thought he was crying because I had broken his toy, but it wasn't that. . . .

"The next time the babysitter came, I spoke with her about discipline. To my surprise or should I say horror, this woman began berating me. She told me what my son needed was a firm hand and I was just going to spoil him if I kept up all that nonsense of non-physical discipline. I fired her on the spot."

Will all the painstaking precautions insure us that the chosen applicant is suitable for the job? As one family found out, no it does not. In their case, despite careful, methodical checking their twenty-one-month-old baby died of brain damage brought on by abuse at the hands of a sixteen-year-old babysitter.

Was it the parents' fault it happened? No. They had followed the book. Should we, therefore, throw out the book?

164

No. We are all doing the best we can, and we must continue to do so.

Conclusion

The healthy development of children hinges on security, trust and love. Having been given the rules of streetproofing, they also must learn the meaning of trust so that they can fully understand what loving really means.

We love best by first loving ourselves. We learn to trust others by first trusting our parents. This is an important element of streetproofing. Learning about sexual abuse prevention requires an element of trust because only those children will "tell" who have found someone they can trust enough to tell.

We can teach trust by respecting and believing in our children. Only by being certain of our trust will they know that no matter what happens — even if they do something terribly wrong — we will never stop loving them.

I wish you luck and a safe life.

Appendix

PARENTING BOOKS

References and Recommended Reading

Bloorview Children's Hospital Sexuality Committee *Making Love, Etc. A Booklet for Young People with Physical Disabilities.* Toronto: Bloorview Children's Hospital, 1985.

Boston Women's Health Book Collective. *Ourselves and Our Children,* New York: Random House, 1978.

Calderone, Mary S., and Ramey, James W., *Talking With Your Child About Sex.* New York: Ballantine Books, 1 9 8 2 .

Caplan, Frank and Caplan, Theresa. *The First Twelve Months of Life; The Second Twelve Months of Life; The Early Childhood Years: The 2 to 6 Year Old.* New York: Bantam Books, 1977.

Dodson, Fitzhugh. *How to Parent.* New York: New American Library, 1973.

Elkind, David. *The Hurried Child.* Reading, Mass: Addison-Wesley Publishing Co., 1981

Featherstone, Heather. *A Difference in the Family, Living With A Disabled Child.* New York: Penguin Books, 1981.

Lewis, Howard, and Lewis, Martha E. *Sex Education Begins at Home.* Englewood, N.J.: Prentice-Hall, 1983.

McArthur, Shirley H. *Raising Your Hearing-Impaired Child: A Guideline for Parents.* Washington, D.C.: Alexander Graham Bell Association for the Deaf, 1982.

Miller, Mary Susan. *Child-Stress: Understanding and Answering Stress Signals of Infants, Children and*

Teenagers. New York: Doubleday & Company, Inc., 1982

Olds, Sally W. *The Working Parents' Survival Guide.* Toronto: Bantam Books, Inc., 1983.

Postman, Neil. *The Disappearance of Childhood.* New York: Dell Publishing Co. Inc., 1982.

Stein, Sara Bonnet, in cooperation with the Children's Television Workshop. *Learn at Home The Sesame Street Way.* (A Fireside Book). New York: Simon and Schuster, 1979.

White, Burton, L. *The First Three Years of Life.* New York: Avon Books, 1975.

SAFETY BOOKS
References and Recommended Reading

*Books For Children

Abrahms, Sally. *Children in the Crossfire: The Tragedy of Parental Kidnapping.* New York: Atheneum Publishers, 1983.

Adams, Caren, and Fay, Jennifer. *No More Secrets: Protecting Your Child From Sexual Assault.* San Luis Obispo, CA: Impact Publishers, 1983.

Adams, Caren, and Fay, Jennifer, and Loreen-Martin, Jan. *No is Not Enough: Helping Teenagers Avoid Sexual Assault.* San Luis Obispo, CA.: Impact Publishers, 1984.

*Brady, Janeen. *Safety Kids: Personal Safety. A Sing-Along Colouring Book.* Brite Music Enterprises, Inc., 1983.

Briggs, Dorothy C. *Your Child's Self-Esteem.* (A Dolphin Book). New York: Doubleday & Co. Inc., 1975.

Brownmiller, Susan. *The Best Kept Secret: Sexual Abuse of Children.* Englewood, N.J.: Prentice-Hall Inc., 1980.

*Cohen, Mary Ann. *Go Safe. Play Safe. Feel Safe. Grow Safe. A Golden Book Series of Activity Books for Young Children.* Racine, Wisc.: Western Publishing Company, Inc., 1985.

Colao, Flora and Hosansky, Tamar. *Your Children Should Know.* New York: Berkeley Books, 1983.

*Dayee, Frances S. *Private Zone: A Book Teaching Children Sexual Assault Prevention Tools.* Edmonds, WA.: The Chas. Franklin Press, Edmonds, 1982.

*Ebert, Jeanne. *What Would You Do If . . . ? A Safety Game For You and Your Child.* Boston, Mass: Houghton Mifflin Co., 1985.

Fay, Jennifer. *He Told Me Not to Tell.* Renton, WA.: King County Rape Relief, 1979.

Gossage, Richard C., and Gunton, Melvin J. *A Parent's Guide to Streetproofing Children.* (A Seal Book). Toronto: McClelland and Stewart, 1982.

*Hall, Barbara, and Hall, Doug. *Playing It Safe: Street Smart Activities for Children.* Toronto: Methuen Publications, 1984.

Kraizer, Sherryll Kerns. *The Safe Child Book.* New York: Dell Publishing Co. Inc., 1985.

*Kyte, Kathy S. *Play It Safe.* New York: Alfred A. Knopf, 1983.

*Lenett, Robin, with Crane, Bob. *It's OK to Say NO! A Parent/Child Manual for the Protection of Children.* New York: Tom Doherty Associates, 1985.

Long, Lynette, and Long, Thomas. *The Handbook for Latchkey Children and Their Parents.* New York: Berkeley Book, 1984.

*Long, Lynette. *On My Own.* Washington, D.C.: Acropolis Book Ltd., 1984.

*Meyer, Linda D. *Safety Zone: A Book Teaching Child Abduction Prevention Skills.* Edmonds, WA.: Chas. Franklin Press, 1984.

National Committee for Prevention of Child Abuse, *1985 NCPCA Catalog listing material pertaining to child abuse.* (Obtainable from: NCPCA, 332 South Michigan Ave., Chicago, Illinois 60604.

Ontario Association of Professional Social Workers, *Child Abuse: A Handbook for Social Workers in Ontario.* Toronto: Ontario Association of Professional Social Workers, 1983.

Rossi, Janie Hart. *Protect Your Child From Sexual Abuse* and *It's My Body.* Seattle, WA.: Parenting Press, Inc., 1984.

Sanford, Linda Tschirhart. *The Silent Children: A Parent's Guide to The Prevention of Child Abuse.* New York: McGraw-Hill Book Co., 1980.

Star, Barbara. *Helping The Abuser: Intervening Effectively in Family Violence.* New York: Family Service Association of America, 1983.

*Williams, Joy. *Red Flag, Green Flag People. A Colouring Book for Young Children.* Fargo-Moorhead, N.D.: Rape and Abuse Crisis Center, 1980.

Wachter, Oralee. *No More Secrets for Me.* Toronto: Little, Brown and Co. (Canada), 1983.